The Indie Artist Playbook

Your Step by Step Guide to a Successful Music Career

PUBLISHED BY: Doug Ross

This book is dedicated to James Palmer-Bullock & Tom Mills

Doug Ross

Contents

The Journey of an Independent Artist

In the early '90s, I remember watching Mix Master Mike from the Beastie Boys cutting and scratching beats on stage as part of their performance. It totally captivated me and inspired me to want to become a DJ and performer. I'm Doug Ross and I'll be your guide through this book. With 25 years of experience working in the music industry, I've had the privilege of touring the world, sharing my music with millions, and earning a living from my passion. My career began as a DJ and producer, releasing tracks that found their way into clubs, onto TV shows, and radio stations. I've performed in front of crowds in the tens of thousands and experienced the highs and lows that come with being an independent artist.

My journey expanded beyond performing. I've been a booking agent, artist manager, tour manager, promoter, A&R rep and event organiser. My true passion lies in discovering talent and helping artists carve out successful, sustainable careers in music. I understand the challenges and triumphs of this path and want to share my insights with you.

This book is more than just a guide; it's a roadmap to help you navigate the often chaotic world of independent music. Whether you're just starting out or looking to elevate your career, my goal is to equip you with the tools, insights, and inspiration you need to make your mark.

So why this book and why now?

I've faced the uncertainty, the long hours, and the tough breaks. But I've also seen dreams come to fruition. Through this book, I want to show you that it's possible to turn your passion into a profitable career.

Honouring Friends: This book is dedicated to some good friends who have passed away in recent years, who dedicated their lives to helping new talent grow and discover their potential. Their legacy inspires me to continue supporting emerging artists.

Bridging the Knowledge Gap: In a world where information is at your fingertips, it's easy to get overwhelmed and not know what to lean into. This book aims to provide guidance on what to focus on and the right paths to take.

Empowering Independent Artists: I want to empower you with my personal insights from 25 years in the industry, offering practical advice, what tools to use and strategies for success.

Staying Up with Industry and Technology Changes: The music industry is constantly evolving. This book provides up-to-date information on the latest trends and technologies.

Creating a Lasting Resource: This book is a resource you can return to time and time again, and share with friends, ensuring you have the support you need throughout your journey.

Each chapter will walk you through a different aspect of being an independent artist. From honing your unique sound and setting up a home studio, to mastering the art of self-promotion and monetising your music, I'll cover it all. I'll share personal stories, practical advice, and actionable steps to help you overcome obstacles and seize opportunities.

You'll find insights into industry trends, tips for building a loyal fanbase, and strategies for leveraging social media to expand your reach. I'll discuss how to navigate the business side of music, from contract negotiations to understanding royalties. This book aims to equip you with the knowledge and tools to not only survive but thrive in the music industry. It's designed to help turn your artistic dreams into reality, providing the guidance and inspiration you need to succeed.

What You'll Gain

Insight: Learn from my experiences and the lessons I've gathered over the years.

Practical Tips: Get straightforward advice on everything from recording to marketing.

Inspiration: Feel motivated to pursue your dreams with confidence and determination.

Tools for Success: Equip yourself with the knowledge and strategies needed to thrive as an independent artist.

My passion lies in helping you succeed. I believe that with the right mindset and resources, you can achieve incredible things. By the end of this book, I hope you'll feel empowered to take your music seriously, make bold moves, and build a career that brings both fulfilment and financial reward.

The Independent Artist's Path

An independent artist crafts, produces, and promotes their music outside the traditional record label system. Unlike artists who sign with major labels, indies take full control of their careers, making decisions about their music, branding, marketing, and distribution.
As an independent artist, you're not just a musician; you're also a businessperson, marketer, social media manager, and sometimes even your own booking agent and tour manager. This level of control allows you to stay true to your artistic vision without external pressures to conform to commercial trends.

I've seen many artists who have signed with major record labels but found themselves with limited control, facing artistic differences, and being pushed in directions that didn't align with their own values and vision. While it works for some, many end up disillusioned, dropped from their label or frustrated. The freedom to create and steer your own career is invaluable.

The independent path is challenging but incredibly rewarding. It offers the freedom to experiment, the ability to connect directly with your audience, and the potential to reap all the financial benefits from your music. You set the pace, make the creative choices, and ultimately, you define your success.

In this book, I'll walk you through the essential components of being an independent artist. My goal is to provide you with practical advice and inspiring stories that will help you navigate the complexities of the independent music scene and achieve your dreams.

Let's go!

Finding Your Sound

Discovering and developing your unique musical style is one of the most crucial steps in your journey as an artist. It's about finding what resonates with you and what makes you stand out in a crowded industry. Here, I'll share some tips and insights from my own experience, as well as industry findings, to help you carve out your musical identity.

Embrace Your Passion

When I first started out, I decided to make the music I loved: Drum and Bass and later cinematic electronic music for TV and video games. This wasn't just a strategic choice—it was about creating something I was passionate about. Passion fuels creativity, and when you're genuinely excited about the music you're making, it shows in your work. So, start by asking yourself: What kind of music makes you feel alive? What genres or styles do you keep coming back to?

Acknowledge Your Limitations

Understanding your strengths and limitations is key to developing your sound. Early in my career, I realised that while I had a knack for creating compelling music, my mixdowns were not as polished as they could be. Instead of letting this hold me back, I sought out engineers who could bring a higher level of expertise to my projects. Recognising where you need help and being willing to seek it out can make a significant difference in the quality of your music.

The Power of Collaboration

Collaboration has been one of the most important aspects of my career. Working with other producers, vocalists, and songwriters not only enhanced my music but also helped me discover new elements of my sound. Each collaborator brings their own unique perspective and skills, enriching your music and helping you explore different directions.

One of the best ways to find your unique sound is to experiment with different collaborators. Don't be afraid to reach out to other artists whose work you admire. Collaboration can push you out of your comfort zone and inspire you to think creatively in ways you might not have considered on your own.

Focus on Your Niche

While it's essential to be open to evolution and growth, having a clear focus is equally important. When you know what you want to achieve and the kind of music you want to create, it gives your work a sense of direction and purpose. For me, this meant focusing on Drum and Bass and cinematic music. Having this focus didn't limit my creativity; rather, it provided a foundation upon which I could build and innovate.

Industry Insights

The music industry is filled with stories of artists who found success by honing their unique sound. For example, think of artists like Billie Eilish or Daft Punk, who each carved out a distinctive style that set them apart. Research shows that having a recognisable sound can help you build a loyal fan base. According to a study by MusicWatch, artists who establish a unique style and brand identity tend to attract more dedicated listeners who are eager to support their music and attend their shows.

Evolution and Adaptation

It's also worth noting that your sound can and likely will evolve over time. As you grow as an artist and gain more experience, your influences and interests may change. This evolution is natural and can lead to exciting new directions in your music. However, even as you evolve, maintaining a core element that is uniquely yours will help keep your sound coherent and recognisable.

Recording Cover Songs: A strategic path to engaging an audience

In the competitive world of music, breaking through the noise with your original work can be challenging. However, one effective strategy to gain engagement and direct listeners to your original music is by recording cover songs. This approach isn't a shortcut or a cheat, but a proven way to showcase your talent and attract a broader audience.

The Power of a Cover Song

Cover songs allow you to tap into the existing fan base of a popular track, providing an immediate audience who is already familiar with and fond of the original. When done creatively, covers can highlight your unique style and vocal quality, encouraging listeners to explore more of your music, including your original songs.

Creative Approaches to Cover Songs

To stand out with your cover, consider these innovative approaches:

Gender Swap: If you're a male artist, try covering a song originally performed by a female artist, and vice versa. This can bring a fresh perspective and a new emotional depth to the song.

Change the Key: Adjusting the key of the song to better suit your vocal range can make your performance more powerful and authentic.

Tempo Adjustments: Slowing down a fast-paced song or speeding up a slow song can dramatically alter its mood and feel, making it uniquely yours.

Unique Arrangements: Experiment with different genres and arrangements. For instance, transforming a pop song into an acoustic ballad or a rock anthem into a jazz standard can capture attention and demonstrate your versatility. Remember, simplicity often works best; a straightforward, heartfelt rendition can be more impactful than an overly complex production.

Selecting the Right Songs

For maximum impact, choose well-known tracks rather than mid-level album cuts. Popular songs have a built-in audience and are more likely to be discovered and shared. Platforms like Spotify and YouTube can help you identify trending tracks that are ripe for covering.

Releasing Your Cover Songs

Once you've recorded your cover, platforms like DistroKid make it easy to distribute your music while handling all necessary licenses. This means you can legally release your cover songs on major streaming services, ensuring you get the credit—and revenue—you deserve. If you don't use DistroKid as your distributor, check with your chosen distributor that they clear all licenses so you don't get into trouble.

The Influence of Media Syncs

Cover songs also have the potential to be featured in popular media, providing another avenue for exposure. Television shows like "Love Island" frequently sync unique cover versions in their episodes, reaching millions of viewers and creating viral moments. Your version could be the next big hit, catapulting your name into the public eye.

Wrap Up

Recording cover songs is a strategic move for any aspiring musician. It not only showcases your talent but also bridges the gap between listeners and your original music. By selecting the right songs and adding your unique twist, you can build a loyal following and pave the way for your original tracks to shine.

Finding your unique sound is a journey, not a destination. It requires self-discovery and a willingness to embrace both your strengths and limitations. By focusing on your passion, seeking out collaborations, and staying true to your vision, you can develop a musical style that is truly your own. Remember, the most successful artists are those who are not afraid to be themselves and let their individuality shine through their music.

Building a home studio on a budget

Creating a home studio is a great way to provide a safe space for your creativity to flourish. Ideally, you'll want a space in your home or garden where you can make noise and record your ideas without interruptions. While recording voice notes and ideas on your phone is convenient, investing in a more robust setup allows you to record instruments and vocals with higher quality, avoiding the costs of studio rentals and hiring engineers. Setting up a home studio can be affordable if you know what equipment to get and where to find it.

The Essentials for a Home Studio

To build an effective home studio on a budget, you'll need to focus on the essentials: a computer, music software (DAW), an audio interface (sound card), and a microphone. Here's a breakdown of each component, along with some examples and tips on where to buy them.

Computer
Your computer is the heart of your home studio. While you don't need the latest model, it should be powerful enough to handle recording software and plugins without lag. Both Mac and PC can work well, depending on your preference and budget.

Examples:
Mac: MacBook Air (M2, 2022) or Mac Mini (M2, 2023)
PC: Dell XPS 8950 or HP Envy Desktop TE01-2275xt (2022)
Where to Look: Check out Amazon, Best Buy (US/Canada), or your local computer store. For second-hand options, consider eBay or Facebook Marketplace.

Music Software (DAW)

A Digital Audio Workstation (DAW) is essential for recording, editing, and producing your music. Many DAWs offer free versions or affordable subscriptions.

Examples:
Free: Audacity, GarageBand (Mac only)
Paid: Logic Pro, Pro Tools or Ableton Live
Where to Look: Official websites of the DAW developers, Amazon, or Sweetwater (USA).

Audio Interface (Sound Card)

An audio interface connects your instruments and microphone to your computer, converting analogue signals to digital.

Examples:
Focusrite Scarlett 2i2
PreSonus AudioBox USB 96
Where to Look: Amazon, Sweetwater (USA). For used options, check eBay, Facebook Marketplace or Reverb.

Microphone

A quality microphone is crucial for recording vocals and instruments. Condenser microphones are generally preferred for their sensitivity and clarity.

Examples:
Audio-Technica AT2020
Rode NT1-A
Where to Look: Amazon, Sweetwater (USA), For second-hand, look on eBay or Facebook Marketplace.

Additional Tips for Building Your Home Studio

Research and Recommendations: Before purchasing, do thorough research on each piece of equipment. Read reviews, watch video tutorials, and ask friends or colleagues in the industry for their recommendations.

Buy Used Equipment: You can save a significant amount of money by buying second-hand equipment. Websites like Facebook Marketplace, eBay, and Reverb are excellent places to find used gear at a fraction of the price of new items.

Start Small and Upgrade Gradually: You don't need to buy everything at once. Start with the essentials and gradually upgrade your setup as your budget allows.

Acoustic Treatment: If possible, invest in some basic acoustic treatment for your recording space. Foam panels, bass traps, and diffusers can significantly improve your recording quality by reducing echo and background noise.

Wrap Up

Setting up a home studio on a budget is entirely feasible with the right approach and research. By focusing on the essential equipment and exploring second-hand options, you can create a space where your creativity can thrive without breaking the bank. Remember, the goal is to have a functional setup that allows you to record your ideas and produce high-quality music from the comfort of your home. Take your time, do your research, and invest wisely. Your future self will thank you.

Songwriting and Composition Techniques

Creating compelling songs and compositions is at the heart of being an independent artist. Whether you're a producer or a songwriter, understanding the techniques that can elevate your music is crucial. In this chapter, we'll explore strategies for both producers and songwriters, share some inspirational stories and quotes from successful artists, and offer practical tips to kickstart your writing process.

For Producers

Producers often focus on the technical and musical aspects of creating a track. Here are some techniques and tips specifically for producers:

Master the Basics

Understanding music theory can significantly enhance your production skills although not essential. I started by learning how to play the piano and achieving my grade 4. This foundation helped me understand keys, tempos, and musical structures, which are essential when making music and collaborating with others. Even if you use modern tools and plugins, a basic knowledge of music theory can help you make more informed creative decisions.

Example: Deadmau5, a renowned electronic music producer, often emphasises the importance of understanding music theory and sound design to create innovative tracks.

Learn Your DAW Inside Out

Proficiency in your music software is essential. I chose Logic Pro, and once I mastered both the musicality and the software, creating music became much easier. Spend time learning all the features and shortcuts of your software to streamline your workflow.

Tip: Take advantage of online tutorials, forums, and user groups for tips and tricks on your specific software. Even now, 20 years later, I'll jump onto YouTube to find new techniques.

Sound Design and Sampling

Experiment with different sounds and samples to create unique textures and tones. Invest time in learning sound design techniques, as this can set your music apart. Make sure any samples you use are cleared before use.

Example: Skrillex is known for his innovative sound design, often creating entirely new sounds by manipulating samples and using creative effects.

Stay Organised

Keep your projects and samples organised. Label your tracks, use colour coding, and maintain a tidy workspace to enhance productivity.

Tip: Use project templates to save time and ensure consistency across your tracks.

Collaborate

Work with other producers, vocalists, and musicians. Collaboration can bring fresh ideas and perspectives to your music. Use tools like cloud-based DAWs or shared note-taking

17

apps to facilitate collaboration. Make sure that you agree royalty splits based on how much effort and input you have made on a track so there is no disputes down the line.

> ## *"Collaboration is key. Some of my best work has come from working with other talented individuals." – Mark Ronson*

For Songwriters

Songwriters focus on crafting lyrics and melodies that resonate with listeners. Here are some strategies and tips for songwriters:

Start with a Concept

Begin with a clear idea or emotion you want to convey. Having a strong concept can guide your writing process and keep your song focused. This central theme will help you maintain coherence throughout the song and ensure that your lyrics and melodies align with the message or story you want to tell.

Example: Taylor Swift often starts with a personal experience or story, which gives her songs an authentic and relatable quality.

Melody and Harmony

Pay attention to your melodies and harmonies. These elements can make your song memorable and emotionally impactful.

Tip: Use a piano or guitar to experiment with different chord progressions and melodies. Record your sessions to capture spontaneous ideas. Nothing should be wasted.

Lyric Writing

Write lyrics that are honest and relatable. Use vivid imagery and storytelling techniques to engage your listeners.

Example: Bob Dylan is renowned for his storytelling and poetic lyrics, which have made his songs timeless.

Edit and Refine

Don't be afraid to revise your work. Great songs often go through multiple drafts before they reach their final form.

Tip: Take breaks between writing sessions to gain new perspectives on your work.

Collaborate

Collaborate with other songwriters and musicians. Sharing ideas and getting feedback can help you improve and finish your songs. This collaborative process can open up new perspectives and techniques you might not have considered on your own. Working with others allows you to tap into their unique skills and experiences, which can enrich your music and inspire creativity.

"Some of the best songs come from collaborative efforts, where each person brings something unique to the table." — Ed Sheeran

Practical Tips for Starting the Writing Process

Log your ideas

Keep a record of your ideas on your phone. Use note-taking apps to jot down lyrics, melodies, or concepts whenever inspiration strikes. Tip: Voice memos are a great tool for capturing spontaneous melodies or riffs.

Stay Flexible

If you hit a creative block on a track, move on to something else. Staying flexible and working on multiple projects can keep your creativity flowing. Tip: Revisit unfinished tracks later with fresh ears; you might find new inspiration.

Collaborate with Notes

Use shared note-taking apps to collaborate with other writers. This allows for real-time feedback and idea sharing, even when you're not in the same location. Example: Google Keep, Evernote, or Apple Notes are excellent tools for this purpose.

Practice regularly

Like any skill, songwriting and composing improve with practice. Set aside dedicated time each day or week to work on your music.

"The more you write, the better you get. Don't wait for inspiration; create a routine." – Paul McCartney

Wrap Up

Whether you're a producer or a songwriter, developing your craft takes time, practice, and a willingness to experiment and collaborate. By mastering the basics, leveraging your software, experimenting with sounds, and working with others, you can create compelling and unique music. Remember to stay organised, keep your ideas logged, and be flexible in your creative process. With dedication and persistence, you'll find your voice and make music that resonates with listeners. Find a couple of trusted friends who are willing to listen to your ideas or demo tracks and provide constructive feedback. Having a reliable support system can be invaluable, as they can offer new perspectives, highlight areas for improvement, and encourage you throughout your creative process. Make sure these friends are honest and supportive, so their input can genuinely help you grow and refine your work.

Recording and Producing Your Music

Recording, mixing, and mastering your tracks are crucial steps in bringing your music to life. Whether you're working in your own home studio or a rented space, understanding each stage of the process will help you produce professional-quality music. Here's a step-by-step guide to recording and producing your tracks, along with some insights into the role of AI in music production.

Step-by-Step Process

Recording into Your Music Software

Setup: Start by setting up your audio interface (sound card) and connecting it to your computer and software. Make sure your microphones, instruments, and other equipment are properly connected and configured.

Recording: Record your instruments and vocals into the software. Ensure you capture clean, high-quality audio by setting appropriate input levels and using good recording techniques. Record multiple takes if necessary.

Example: Using an audio interface like the Focusrite Scarlett 2i2 and software such as Logic Pro or Ableton Live.

Editing the Audio

Initial Edit: Review your recorded tracks and start editing. Trim any unwanted noise, and delete or silence mistakes.

Re-record if Necessary: If any parts are unsatisfactory, re-record those sections until you get the desired take.

Adding New Sections: Layer in additional parts, such as harmonies, double tracks, or chorus sections, to build a fuller sound.

Comping: Compile the best parts from multiple takes into a single, seamless track.

Tuning Vocals

Software Tools: Use vocal tuning software to correct pitch and timing issues. Free tools like Auto-Tune Free or GSnap can help, while paid options like Melodyne or Antares Auto-Tune provide more advanced features.

Tips: Aim for a natural sound. Over-tuning can make vocals sound robotic unless that's the effect you want.

Mixing the Elements

Balancing Levels: Adjust the volume levels of each track to ensure a balanced mix where no single element overpowers the others. Mixing levels should NEVER go above 0db.

EQ and Compression: Use equalization (EQ) to carve out space for each instrument and apply compression to control dynamics and add consistency. This takes a lot of practice.

Adding Effects: Apply effects like reverb, delay, and modulation to enhance the sound. Be mindful of not overdoing it—subtlety is key otherwise your sound will sound like mush.

Automation: Automate volume, pan, and effects parameters to create dynamic changes throughout your track.

Mastering the Track

Final Polish: Mastering is the final step where you prepare your mix for distribution. It involves EQ adjustments, compression, limiting, and ensuring the track meets industry loudness standards. You can do this with practice or outsource to a professional.

Software Tools: Use mastering software or plugins such as iZotope Ozone or Waves Mastering Suite.

DIY vs Professional: While you can master your tracks yourself, hiring a professional mastering engineer can provide a fresh perspective and polish.

Research and Skill Development

If you're not familiar with any of these areas, invest time in learning and practicing. There are numerous resources available online, including tutorials, forums, and courses on platforms like YouTube, Coursera, and Udemy. Also, don't hesitate to seek advice from friends or industry professionals.

The Role of AI in Music Production

Artificial Intelligence (AI) is transforming the music production landscape, offering tools and solutions to streamline various aspects of the process:

AI for Mixing and Mastering

Mixing: AI-powered plugins like iZotope Neutron can automatically analyse your mix and suggest adjustments for EQ, compression, and other effects.

Mastering: AI mastering services like LANDR or eMastered offer quick, affordable mastering solutions by analysing your tracks and applying industry-standard mastering techniques.

AI for Composition and Arrangement

Composition Tools: AI-driven platforms like Amper Music or AIVA can help you generate musical ideas and arrangements, providing a starting point for your compositions.

Example: Taryn Southern's album "I AM AI" was co-produced with AI, showcasing how AI can assist in creating music. We are seeing this more and more.

AI for Vocal Processing

Tuning and Editing: AI-enhanced vocal tuning software like iZotope Nectar offers advanced features for pitch correction, harmonizing, and vocal effects.

AI for Sound Design

Sound Generation: Tools like Google's Magenta or OpenAI's MuseNet use AI to generate new sounds and musical ideas, which can inspire your production. Worth checking out.

While AI tools can significantly enhance your workflow, they are not a replacement for human creativity and intuition. Use them as aids to complement your skills and streamline repetitive tasks, allowing you to focus more on the creative aspects of your music.

Wrap Up

Recording, mixing, and mastering your music are essential skills for any independent artist. These processes are the backbone of producing professional-sounding tracks and can significantly impact how your music is perceived by listeners. By understanding the step-by-step process, investing in the right tools, and continually learning and adapting, you can produce high-quality tracks from your home studio. If you collaborate with other producers or songwriters make sure that you agree splits so there are no disputes down the line.

Embrace the potential of AI tools to enhance your production capabilities. AI-powered plugins and software can assist with tasks like auto-tuning, beat matching, and even generating musical ideas. However, it's essential to use these tools to complement your skills, not replace them. Always keep your creative vision at the forefront, ensuring that your unique style and voice shine through.

The music production landscape is constantly evolving, with new techniques, tools, and trends emerging regularly. Stay updated by following industry blogs, taking online courses, and participating in forums. Networking with other musicians and producers can also provide valuable insights and opportunities for collaboration.

With dedication and practice, you'll be able to bring your musical ideas to life and share them with the world. The journey might be challenging, but each step you take enhances your skills and brings you closer to your goals. Celebrate your progress, learn from your mistakes, and keep pushing your creative boundaries. By mastering these essential skills and leveraging the latest technology, you'll be well-equipped to produce and release music that truly represents your artistic vision.

Releasing Your Music Independently

Releasing your music independently offers unparalleled control over your work and the potential for significant financial returns. This chapter will guide you through the process of distributing your music on various platforms, building a fan base, and maximising your income from different revenue streams.

Platforms for Independent Music Release

There are several platforms where you can release your music independently. Here's a breakdown of the most popular ones:

Spotify

Overview: Spotify is one of the largest music streaming platforms, offering vast exposure to listeners worldwide. Setting up a Spotify for Artists account allows you to manage your profile, submit songs for playlist consideration, and access valuable analytics.

Distribution: Use a distribution service like DistroKid, TuneCore, or CD Baby to get your music on Spotify. These services ensure your tracks are available globally hassle free.

Promotion: Building relationships with indie playlist curators and actively promoting your music on social media are crucial steps for gaining streams. While there's a small chance Spotify might add your song to their playlists, proactive promotion is 100% essential.

Apple Music

Overview: Apple Music is another major streaming platform with a huge user base. Setting up an Apple Music for Artists account helps you manage your profile and track your performance.

Distribution: Similar to Spotify, use a distribution service to release your music on Apple Music. Apple Music however doesn't have the same playlist opportunities.

Revenue: Selling your music on iTunes (part of Apple Music) allows listeners to purchase your tracks, providing a higher income per sale compared to streaming revenue. Sadly the ratio of people streaming for Free is significantly higher vs someone buying music.

Bandcamp

Overview: Bandcamp is a platform focused on supporting independent artists by allowing them to sell their music directly to fans. You can offer digital downloads, physical merchandise, and even vinyl records.

Promotion: Bandcamp is great for building a dedicated fan base. Engage with your fans by sharing updates, offering exclusive content, and utilising Bandcamp's robust community features.

Revenue: Bandcamp takes a small commission on sales, but the majority of the revenue goes directly to the artist. This makes it a highly lucrative platform for independent musicians.

Patreon

Overview: Patreon is a membership platform where fans can support your work through monthly subscriptions. In return, you provide them with exclusive content, early access to new music, and other perks.

Promotion: Building a loyal fan base is key to success on Patreon. Regularly engage with your patrons and offer valuable, exclusive content to maintain and grow your subscriber base.

Revenue: Patreon offers a steady stream of income, allowing you to fund your music projects through the direct support of your fans.

Importance of a Fan Base

Having a dedicated fan base is crucial for the success of your independent music career. Streams and listens don't happen magically; they result from strategic promotion and engagement with your audience. Here's how to build and maintain a fan base:

Social Media Engagement

Use platforms like Instagram, X, TikTok, and Facebook to connect with your audience. Share behind-the-scenes content, engage with your followers, and promote your music releases. They want to hear from you.

Email Marketing

Build an email list to keep your fans updated on new releases, upcoming shows, and exclusive content. Email marketing is one of the most powerful tools still for maintaining direct communication with your audience.

Live Performances

Perform live, whether in-person or through live-streaming platforms. Live performances help you connect with your fans and attract new listeners. Performing live also continues to be one of the best ways to generate an income as an independent artists through selling merchandise. This could be a Vinyl, CD or Tape of your latest EP/Album or giving your new fans a unique piece of memorabilia.

Setting Up Accounts and Distribution

To release your music, you'll need to set up accounts on various platforms and choose a distribution service. This process is essential for getting your music out to the world and ensuring it reaches your audience effectively. Here's a step-by-step guide to help you navigate this crucial phase:

Choose a Distribution Service

Select a distribution service like DistroKid, TuneCore, or CD Baby. These services will distribute your music to Spotify, Apple Music, and other major streaming platforms at the click of a few buttons.

Steps:
- Sign up for an account.
- Upload your music, artwork, and metadata.
- Select the platforms you want your music to be distributed to.
- Pay the distribution fee (if applicable) and submit your release.

Set Up Artist Accounts

Spotify for Artists

- Sign up at artists.spotify.com
- Claim your artist profile and verify your identity.

- Customise your profile with a bio, photos, and social media links.

Apple Music for Artists

- Sign up at artists.apple.com
- Claim your artist profile and verify your identity.
- Customise your profile and review your analytics.

Bandcamp

- Sign up at bandcamp.com
- Create your artist profile and upload your music and artwork.
- Set pricing for your music and merchandise.

Patreon

- Sign up at patreon.com
- Create your artist profile and set up membership tiers.
- Offer exclusive content and perks to attract subscribers.

Prepare Your Music for Release

Final Edits: Ensure your tracks are mixed and mastered to the highest quality.

Metadata: Include all necessary metadata such as song titles, artist name, album name, and genre.

Artwork: Create professional cover art that represents your music and brand. Sites like fiverr can create artwork at low costs.

Promotional Plan: Develop a promotional plan that includes social media campaigns, email newsletters, and press releases.

Revenue Streams and Promotion

Understanding the differences in revenue streams from various platforms is crucial:

Streaming vs. Sales

Streaming: Platforms like Spotify and Apple Music pay per stream, which is often a fraction of a pence. While this can add up with a large number of streams, it's generally less lucrative than direct sales.

Sales: Selling your music on platforms like Bandcamp or iTunes allows you to earn more per sale. For example, selling a track for £1 on Bandcamp can generate more income than thousands of streams on Spotify.

Patreon Subscriptions

Patreon offers a consistent income through monthly subscriptions. By offering exclusive content and perks, you can build a reliable revenue stream from your most dedicated fans.

Role of AI in Promotion and Distribution

AI is playing an increasingly important role in music promotion and distribution:

AI-Driven Playlisting

Services like Spotify use AI to curate playlists based on listening habits. Getting your song on these playlists can significantly boost your exposure and income.

Automated Marketing

AI tools can help automate your marketing efforts. Platforms like Hootsuite or Buffer allow you to schedule and analyse social media posts, making it easier to manage your promotional activities.

Data Analysis

AI can analyse listener data to help you understand your audience better. This insight allows you to tailor your marketing strategies and improve engagement.

Wrap Up

Releasing your music independently gives you the freedom to control your career and maximise your earnings. By leveraging various platforms and understanding the importance of a dedicated fan base, you can successfully distribute your music globally. Remember to research each platform, build strong promotional strategies, and continuously engage with your audience. With dedication and the right tools, you can achieve success as an independent artist.

Creating a Memorable Brand Identity and Visual Style

In the music industry, building a strong brand identity is as crucial as the music itself. Your brand encompasses not only your sound but also your visual style, public persona, and the values you convey to your audience. This chapter explores how to craft a memorable brand identity and visual style, with examples of iconic music artists who have successfully leveraged their brand to achieve enduring fame.

Understanding Brand Identity for Music Artists

Defining Your Core Values and Vision
Your core values and vision form the foundation of your brand identity. They represent what you stand for and guide your artistic direction and public persona.

Example: Beyoncé - Beyoncé's brand is built on themes of empowerment, feminism, and artistic excellence. Her core values are reflected in her music, performances, and public statements, creating a powerful brand identity.

Crafting Your Personal Narrative
Your story is a crucial element of your brand. Sharing your journey, struggles, and triumphs helps build an emotional connection with your audience.

Example: Eminem - Eminem's brand is deeply tied to his personal narrative of overcoming adversity. His lyrics often reflect his troubled upbringing, battles with addiction, and path to success, creating a raw and authentic brand.

Developing a Visual Style

Consistency in Visual Elements
Consistency across your visual elements helps reinforce your brand identity. This includes your album covers, music videos, stage design, and merchandise.

Example: Lady Gaga - Lady Gaga's visual style is characterised by bold, avant-garde fashion and dramatic performances. Her consistent use of extravagant costumes and innovative stage setups reinforces her brand as a trailblazer in pop culture.

Creating Signature Elements
Developing signature visual elements can make your brand instantly recognisable. These can be specific fashion choices, symbols, or recurring themes in your visuals.

Example: Prince - Prince's use of the color purple, his unique fashion sense, and the iconic "Love Symbol" became his signature elements, making his brand instantly recognisable and synonymous with his music.

Building a Cohesive Online Presence

Website and Social Media
Your online presence is a vital part of your brand. Your website should reflect your brand's visual style and serve as a central hub for your music, tour dates, and news. Social media platforms are essential for engaging with fans and sharing content that aligns with your brand.

Example: Taylor Swift - Taylor Swift's online presence is meticulously curated to reflect her evolving brand. From her website to her Instagram feed, every element is consistent with her current album's aesthetic and narrative.

Music Videos and Visual Content
Music videos and other visual content provide opportunities to express your brand identity creatively. They should complement your music and reinforce your brand's themes and aesthetics.

Example: Billie Eilish - Billie Eilish's music videos are known for their distinctive, often eerie visuals that reflect her unique artistic vision. Her consistent use of dark, haunting imagery has become a hallmark of her brand.

Live Performances and Public Appearances

Stage Design and Performance Style
Your live performances are a direct extension of your brand. Consider how your stage design, choreography, and overall performance style align with your brand identity.

Example: Daft Punk - Daft Punk's brand identity is heavily tied to their futuristic, robot personas. Their live performances, complete with elaborate light shows and signature helmets, reinforce their brand's techno-centric aesthetic.

Fashion and Public Image
Your fashion choices and public image play a significant role in your brand identity. Consistent and distinctive fashion can make a lasting impression on your audience.

Example: David Bowie - David Bowie's ever-evolving fashion and personas, from Ziggy Stardust to the Thin White Duke, were integral to his brand. His bold, avant-garde fashion choices kept his image fresh and intriguing.

Authenticity and Evolution

Staying True to Your Brand
While it's important to evolve, staying true to your core values and vision is essential. Authenticity resonates with audiences and builds lasting loyalty.

Example: Adele - Adele's brand is built on authenticity, emotional depth, and vocal prowess. Despite evolving musically, she remains true to her core values of honesty and emotional storytelling.

Adapting and Evolving
As you grow as an artist, your brand can evolve. This doesn't mean abandoning your original identity but rather allowing it to mature and expand naturally.

Example: Madonna - Madonna's brand is synonymous with reinvention. Throughout her career, she has continuously evolved her image and sound while maintaining her core identity as a provocative and boundary-pushing artist.

Wrap Up

Creating a memorable brand identity and visual style as a music artist involves a blend of self-awareness, consistency, and strategic presentation. By defining your core values, developing a distinctive visual style, building a cohesive online presence, and staying true to your authentic self while allowing for evolution, you can build a brand that not only enhances your music but also deeply connects with your audience. Use the examples of iconic music artists as inspiration, but always ensure your brand reflects your unique artistic voice.

Creating a Professional Artist Website

In today's digital age, having a professional website is essential for any artist looking to build a strong brand and reach a wider audience. A well-designed website serves as your online portfolio, a hub for your content, and a platform for selling merchandise and engaging with fans. This chapter will guide you through the importance of having a website, tips for designing and maintaining it, and practical steps for setting it up, including cost considerations.

The Importance of a Professional Website

Central Hub for Your Content

Your website is the central location where fans, industry professionals, and potential collaborators can learn about you and your work. It consolidates your music, videos, bio, tour dates, and news in one easily accessible place.

Control Over Your Brand

Unlike social media platforms, a website gives you complete control over how your brand is presented. You can customise the design, content, and layout to reflect your unique artistic vision.

Monetisation Opportunities

A website allows you to sell merchandise, tickets, and music directly to your fans. This direct-to-consumer approach increases your revenue and helps build a closer relationship with your audience.

Professionalism and Credibility

Having a professional website enhances your credibility as an artist. It shows that you are serious about your career and provides a polished, professional image to the world. It also serves as a reliable platform for fans, industry professionals, and potential collaborators to learn more about your work and achievements

Tips for Designing and Maintaining Your Website

Keep It Simple and User-Friendly
Your website should be easy to navigate, with a clean and intuitive design. Prioritise essential information and ensure that visitors can quickly find what they are looking for.

Responsive Design

Make sure your website is mobile-friendly. A responsive design adjusts to different screen sizes, providing an optimal viewing experience on desktops, tablets, and smartphones.

High-Quality Visuals and Content

Use high-quality images, videos, and audio files. Professional photos, album artwork, and well-produced videos create a strong visual impact and enhance your brand.

Regular Updates

Keep your website updated with fresh content. Regularly post news, upcoming events, new releases, and blog updates to keep your audience engaged.

SEO Optimisation

Optimise your website for search engines to increase visibility. Use relevant keywords in your content, meta descriptions, and titles to improve your search engine ranking. Unsure what SEO is. Research and watch tutorials.

Setting Up Your Website: Practical Steps

Choosing a Platform

There are several off-the-shelf website builders that make it easy to create a professional website without needing extensive technical skills. Some popular options include:

Wix: Known for its drag-and-drop interface and flexibility. Offers various templates and customisation options.

Squarespace: Offers sleek, modern designs and is great for artists looking for a visually appealing site.

WordPress: Highly customisable with a wide range of themes and plugins. Requires a bit more technical know-how but offers extensive capabilities.

Bandzoogle: Specifically designed for musicians, offering music-specific features like EPKs (Electronic Press Kits), fan subscriptions, and built-in store functionality.

Costs of Building and Maintaining a Website

Initial Setup Costs: Depending on the platform, the initial setup costs can range from free (with limited features) to around £10-£20 per month for premium plans. Custom domains typically cost £10-£15 per year.

Ongoing Costs: Monthly subscription fees for website builders range from £10 to £30 per month, depending on the features and level of customisation you need. E-commerce functionality may add an additional cost.

Getting a URL and Website Name

Choose a Domain Name: Select a domain name that reflects your artist name or brand. Keep it simple, memorable, and easy to spell.

Check Availability: Use domain registration sites like GoDaddy, Namecheap, or Google Domains to check the availability of your chosen domain.

Register Your Domain: Once you find an available domain, register it through a domain registrar. This typically costs £10-£15 per year.

Connect Your Domain: Follow the instructions provided by your website builder to connect your domain to your website.

Essential Elements for a Music Artist's Website

Homepage
Your homepage should provide a clear introduction to who you are and what you do. Include a professional photo, a brief bio, and links to your latest releases or news.

About Page
Provide a detailed bio, including your background, influences, and career highlights. This helps visitors understand your journey and connect with your story.

Music and Videos
Create dedicated pages for your music and videos. Embed your tracks from platforms like Spotify, Apple Music, or SoundCloud,

and upload high-quality music videos or live performance recordings.

Tour Dates
Keep an up-to-date list of your upcoming performances. Include dates, locations, and links to purchase tickets.

Merchandise Store
Set up an online store to sell merchandise such as t-shirts, posters, vinyl records, and digital downloads. Integrate payment options like PayPal, Stripe, or credit card processing.

Contact Information
Include a contact form or email address for booking inquiries, press requests, and fan messages. Consider adding links to your social media profiles.

Benefits of Having Your Own Website

Direct Fan Engagement

Having your own website offers a unique opportunity to interact directly with your fans without the interference of social media algorithms. On your website, you can build and manage an email list to keep your followers updated on your latest news, releases, and events. Offering exclusive content, such as behind-the-scenes videos, early access to tickets, or special merchandise, can create a deeper connection with your audience. This direct line of communication helps in fostering a loyal fanbase and creates a community centred around your brand.

Data Ownership

When you have your own website, you gain complete control over your data. Unlike social media platforms where data is often shared or sold to third parties, your website allows you to track visitor analytics and gather valuable insights about your audience. This information can be used to understand visitor behaviour, preferences, and trends. By leveraging this data, you can make informed, data-driven decisions to grow your fanbase, tailor your content to their interests, and enhance their overall experience on your site.

Professional Image

A well-maintained website is essential for projecting a professional image. It serves as a central hub for your brand, showcasing your work, achievements, and upcoming projects in a polished manner. This can be particularly valuable when approaching industry professionals, booking agents, and potential collaborators. A professional website demonstrates your commitment and seriousness about your career, making a positive impression and potentially opening doors to new opportunities.

Revenue Generation

Owning a website allows you to create multiple revenue streams by selling merchandise, tickets, and music directly to your audience. This not only increases your earnings but also reduces your reliance on third-party platforms, which often take a significant cut of your profits. By managing sales through your website, you have full control over the customer experience, from product presentation to payment processing, ensuring a seamless and satisfying transaction for your fans.

Wrap Up

Creating a professional artist website is a vital step in building your brand and expanding your reach. By choosing the right platform, keeping your design simple and user-friendly, and regularly updating your content, you can create a compelling online presence that enhances your career. With the added benefits of direct fan engagement, data ownership, and additional revenue opportunities, your website can become a powerful tool in your artistic journey. Take inspiration from the examples and tips provided in this chapter, and start building a website that truly represents your unique vision and brand.

Utilising Social Media for Promotion

In today's digital age, social media is an indispensable tool for music artists looking to grow their audience and promote their work. Platforms like Instagram, Facebook, X, and TikTok offer unique opportunities to connect with fans, share content, and build a loyal following. This chapter explores best practices for using these platforms, strategies for organic growth, the benefits of paid advertising, and tools for managing multiple social media accounts. We will also delve into creative content ideas to make a splash in a saturated online space.

Best Practices for Social Media Platforms

Instagram

Visual Appeal: Instagram is a visually driven platform, so high-quality photos and videos are essential. Use it to share behind-the-scenes content, music video teasers, and concert photos.

Stories and Reels: Utilise Stories for daily updates and Reels for short, engaging videos that showcase your personality and music.

Hashtags: Use relevant hashtags to increase the visibility of your posts. Tools like Hashtagify can help you find popular hashtags in your niche. Always tag in collaborators, band members or brand partners.

Engagement: Respond to comments, participate in Q&A sessions, and engage with fans through direct messages to build a strong community.

Facebook

Page vs. Profile: Create a professional artist page to separate your personal life from your music career.

Events: Use Facebook Events to promote gigs and virtual concerts. Invite your followers and encourage them to share the event.

Content Variety: Mix up your posts with videos, live streams, status updates, and photo albums to keep your audience engaged.

Groups: Join and participate in music-related groups to network with other artists and potential fans.

TikTok

Viral Potential: TikTok's algorithm favors creative and engaging content, making it possible for anyone to go viral.

Challenges and Trends: Participate in popular challenges and trends to reach a wider audience.

Music Clips: Share clips of your songs, behind-the-scenes footage, and funny or relatable content.

Duets and Collaborations: Engage with other creators through duets and collaborations to expand your reach.

X (Formerly Twitter)

Real-Time Updates: Use X for real-time updates, tour announcements, and sharing news articles or reviews about your music.

Engagement: Re-post fan content, reply to messages, and use polls to interact with your followers.

Trending Topics: Participate in trending hashtags and music discussions to increase your visibility.

Short and Sweet: Keep messages concise and impactful, leveraging the character limit to your advantage.

Growing Your Fan Base Organically

Consistent Posting

Consistency is essential for maintaining and expanding your social media presence. By regularly sharing content, you keep your audience engaged and informed about your latest activities. Create a content calendar to schedule your posts in advance, ensuring you remain active across all platforms. This approach helps maintain a steady stream of content that can include updates, behind-the-scenes glimpses, announcements, and more. Regular posting not only keeps your current followers engaged but also attracts new ones by showcasing your dedication and activity.

Authentic Engagement

Interacting authentically with your followers is crucial for building a loyal fanbase. Responding to comments, engaging in meaningful conversations, and showing genuine appreciation for fan support can significantly enhance your connection with your audience. This authenticity fosters trust and loyalty, as fans feel valued and heard. Whether it's liking comments, responding to messages, or participating in discussions, your active presence can turn casual followers into dedicated fans who feel personally connected to you and your work.

Collaborations

Collaborating with other artists and influencers within your genre can be a powerful strategy for organic growth. Cross-promotions and joint projects introduce your work to new audiences and lend additional credibility to your brand. Whether it's co-writing a song, featuring on each other's tracks, or participating in joint social media challenges, these collaborations can significantly expand your reach. By tapping into each other's fanbases, you can mutually benefit from increased visibility and engagement.

User-Generated Content

Encouraging fans to create and share content related to your music is a highly effective way to engage your audience and expand your reach. Invite your fans to share their covers of your songs, create fan art, write reviews, or post about their concert experiences. By reposting and highlighting this user-generated content on your platforms, you not only show appreciation for your fans' efforts but also utilise their networks to reach new potential followers. This type of content is authentic and relatable, often leading to higher engagement rates.

Live Streams

Hosting live streams is an excellent way to interact with your audience in real time. Use live sessions to perform, answer fan questions, share updates, and provide exclusive content. Live streaming creates a sense of immediacy and intimacy, allowing fans to feel like they are part of a special event. This real-time interaction helps build a stronger community and allows you to connect with your audience on a more personal level. Live streams can also be a great platform to debut new material, gather feedback, and create memorable experiences for your fans.

Utilising Paid Advertising

Targeted Ads

Platforms like Facebook, Instagram, and X offer powerful ad targeting options. You can target ads based on demographics, interests, and behaviours to reach potential fans who are most likely to enjoy your music.

Ad Formats

Facebook and Instagram: Use Stories ads, carousel ads, and video ads to showcase your music and drive traffic to your website or streaming platforms.

X: Promote messages or use video ads to increase visibility and engagement.

TikTok: Utilise In-Feed ads, Branded Hashtag Challenges, and TopView ads to capture the attention of TikTok users.

Ad Tools

Facebook Ads Manager: A comprehensive tool for creating, managing, and analysing your ad campaigns on Facebook and Instagram.

X Ads: X's ad platform allows you to promote messages and accounts to reach a broader audience.

TikTok Ads: TikTok's ad platform offers various formats to suit your promotional needs, with options for detailed targeting.

Budgeting

Start with a small budget and gradually increase it based on the performance of your ads. Monitor metrics such as click-through rate (CTR), engagement, and conversions to optimise your campaigns.

Tools for Managing Social Media Accounts

Social Media Management Tools

Hootsuite: Schedule posts, monitor mentions, and analyse performance across multiple social media platforms.

Buffer: Plan and schedule your social media posts in advance, with analytics to track engagement and reach.

Later: Specifically designed for Instagram, Later allows you to plan and schedule posts, and provides insights into your account's performance.

Sprout Social: Offers robust scheduling, engagement, and analytics features to manage your social media presence effectively.

Content Creation Tools

Canva: Create visually appealing graphics and videos for your social media posts with easy-to-use templates.

Adobe Spark: Design eye-catching visuals and videos with professional templates tailored for social media.

Making Noise in a Saturated Online Space

Unique Content

Create content that stands out by being true to your unique style and voice. Authenticity and originality resonate more with audiences than imitating trends.

Engaging Content Ideas

Cover Songs: Recording and filming cover songs can attract fans of the original artists and showcase your musical talent.

Behind-the-Scenes: Share glimpses into your creative process, rehearsals, and daily life as an artist.

Storytelling: Use your posts to tell stories about your songs, lyrics, and experiences in the music industry.

Interactive Content: Create polls, quizzes, and Q&A sessions to engage your audience and encourage participation.

Leveraging Trends

Staying current with social media trends and adapting them to your style is a great way to boost your visibility and attract new followers. Social media platforms are dynamic, with new challenges, memes, and viral trends emerging regularly. By keeping an eye on these trends and finding creative ways to incorporate them into your content, you can tap into larger conversations and reach broader audiences. Whether it's participating in a popular dance challenge, creating a meme that resonates with your brand, or using trending hashtags, aligning with current trends can make your posts more discoverable and engaging. This approach keeps your content fresh and relevant, demonstrating your adaptability and creativity to potential followers.

Fan Involvement

Involving your fans in your creative journey can significantly enhance their connection to you and your work. By seeking their input on aspects such as song choices, album artwork, and tour locations, you make them feel like valued contributors. This involvement can be facilitated through social media polls, Q&A sessions, and interactive posts where fans share their opinions and ideas. When fans see their suggestions considered, it fosters a sense of ownership and investment in your success. This deeper connection strengthens their loyalty and creates a more engaged, active fanbase. By making fans feel integral to your journey, you build a community that is supportive, enthusiastic, and more likely to spread the word about your music.

Benefits of Having Your Own Website

Central Hub

A website acts as a central hub for all your online activities, consolidating your social media presence, music, videos, and merchandise in one place. This comprehensive platform allows fans to easily access everything related to you without navigating through various sites. By providing a one-stop destination, you simplify the user experience, making it more convenient for your audience to stay updated with your latest news, releases, and events. Additionally, a centralised hub can include a blog or news section, further engaging your fans with regular updates and personal insights.

SEO Benefits

Having a website improves your search engine visibility, making it easier for new fans to discover you. By optimising your site with relevant keywords, meta tags, and high-quality content, you can enhance your ranking on search engines like Google. This increased visibility helps attract organic traffic from people searching for related music, genres, or topics. Incorporating a blog with regular posts about your music journey, industry trends, and other relevant content can also boost your SEO efforts. Over time, a well-optimised website can significantly expand your reach and introduce your music to a broader audience.

Email List Building

Use your website to build an email list for direct communication with your fans. Email marketing is a powerful tool for announcing new releases, tours, and exclusive content. By offering incentives such as free downloads, exclusive tracks, or early access to tickets in exchange for email sign-ups, you can grow your list effectively. Regular newsletters keep your audience engaged and informed, fostering a closer relationship. Unlike social media, where algorithms control who sees your posts, emails go directly to your fans' inboxes, ensuring your messages are received and increasing the likelihood of engagement and support.

Professional Image

A well-designed website enhances your professional image and provides a platform where you can present yourself exactly how you want to be seen. It showcases your brand consistently and professionally, which is crucial when attracting industry professionals, booking agents, and potential collaborators. A polished website can include high-quality photos, a detailed biography, press releases, and a portfolio of your work, all tailored to reflect your artistic vision and achievements. This professional presentation not only impresses visitors but also builds credibility and trust, making it easier to establish and grow your career in the music industry.

Wrap Up

Social media is a powerful tool for music artists to grow their audience and promote their work. By following best practices on platforms like Instagram, Facebook, X, and TikTok, you can build a loyal fan base both organically and through paid advertising. Utilise social media management tools to streamline your efforts and ensure consistent, engaging content. In a saturated online space, creativity and authenticity will help you stand out and connect with your audience on a deeper level. Combining your social media strategy with a professional website will further solidify your online presence and support your journey as a successful music artist.

Engaging with Your Audience

Engaging with your audience is a crucial aspect of building a successful music career. The landscape of fan engagement has dramatically evolved over the past two decades. With the birth of social media platforms like Facebook and Myspace around 20 years ago, the ways in which artists connect with their fans have transformed significantly. Today, it is easier than ever to engage with an audience and build a loyal following. This chapter explores techniques for connecting with fans, strategies for effective engagement, and ideas for maintaining a devoted fanbase.

The Evolution of Fan Engagement

From Myspace to Modern Social Media

In the early 2000s, platforms like Myspace and the newly launched Facebook began revolutionising how we artists interacted with our fans. These platforms provided a space for artists to share music, updates, and interact with fans in a way that was previously unimaginable. Fast forward to today, and the options for engagement have expanded exponentially. With the rise of Instagram, Twitter, TikTok, and more, artists now have a multitude of tools at their disposal to connect with their audience on a deeper level.

The Modern Landscape

Modern social media platforms offer real-time interaction, multimedia sharing, and advanced analytics, making it easier to understand and cater to your audience's preferences. These platforms allow for direct communication with fans, personalised content, and the ability to build a community around your music.

Strategies for Engaging with Your Audience

Authenticity and Transparency

Fans appreciate authenticity. Sharing personal stories, behind-the-scenes content, and honest updates about your journey can create a genuine connection with your audience. Transparency about your creative process, struggles, and achievements makes you more relatable and trustworthy.

Consistent Interaction

Regular interaction with your fans keeps them engaged and interested in your work. Respond to comments, participate in conversations, and show appreciation for their support. Consistency in engagement helps maintain a strong connection with your audience.

Exclusive Content

Offer exclusive content to your most dedicated fans. This can include early access to new music, remixes, behind-the-scenes footage, or special live streams. Exclusive content makes fans feel valued and incentivises them to stay connected with you.

Storytelling

Use storytelling to create a deeper connection with your fans. Share the stories behind your songs, your inspiration, and your journey as an artist. Storytelling can make your music more meaningful to your audience and create a lasting impact.

Fan Involvement

Involve your fans in your creative process. Ask for their input on song choices, album artwork, and even setlists for performances.

This not only makes fans feel valued but also strengthens their emotional investment in your music.

Ideas for Engaging with Your Fanbase

Social Media Challenges

Create and participate in social media challenges. These challenges can be related to your music or just for fun. Encourage your fans to participate and share their experiences. Social media challenges can increase your visibility and engagement.

Live Streams and Q&A Sessions

Host live streams and Q&A sessions regularly. Perform live, answer fan questions, and share updates. Live interactions create a sense of community and allow for real-time engagement with your audience.

Fan Contests and Giveaways

Organise fan contests and giveaways. This can include contests for fan art, cover songs, or creative videos related to your music. Offer prizes like signed merchandise, concert tickets, or exclusive content. Contests and giveaways can boost engagement and reward loyal fans.

Collaborations and Features

Collaborate with other artists and feature fan content. Working with other musicians can introduce you to new audiences, while featuring fan content shows appreciation and encourages more fan interaction.

Personalised Messages

Send personalised messages to your fans. Whether it's a thank you note, birthday greeting, or a response to a message, personal touches can make fans feel special and appreciated.

Behind-the-Scenes Content

Share behind-the-scenes content regularly. Show your fans what goes into making your music, from studio sessions to rehearsals and tour preparations. Behind-the-scenes content gives fans a glimpse into your life as an artist and keeps them engaged.

Fan Clubs and Memberships

Create fan clubs or membership programs. Offer exclusive content, early access to tickets, and special merchandise to members. Fan clubs and memberships can create a sense of belonging and loyalty among your fans.

Keeping Fans Coming Back

Regular Content Updates

Keep your content fresh and updated. Regularly post new music, videos, updates, and interactive content. Consistent updates keep your fans interested and coming back for more.

Interactive Content

Create interactive content such as polls, quizzes, and challenges. Interactive content encourages fans to engage with your posts and can be a fun way to connect with your audience.

Acknowledging Fans

Show appreciation for your fans' support. Acknowledge their contributions, share their content, and thank them publicly. Acknowledging fans makes them feel valued and strengthens their loyalty.

Engaging Performances

Ensure that your live performances, whether virtual or in-person, are engaging and memorable. High-energy shows, audience interaction, and unique performances can leave a lasting impression on your fans.

Building a Community

Foster a sense of community among your fans. Encourage them to interact with each other, share their experiences, and support each other. Building a community around your music can create a loyal and supportive fanbase.

What Makes a Loyal Fan

Emotional Connection

Loyal fans often have an emotional connection to your music and your story. By sharing your journey and creating meaningful content, you can build a strong emotional bond with your audience.

Exclusive Access

Providing exclusive access to content, events, and merchandise can make fans feel special and valued. Exclusive access creates a sense of privilege and deepens fan loyalty.

Consistent Engagement

Consistently engaging with your fans shows that you care about them and appreciate their support. Regular interaction and acknowledgment help build a strong and loyal fanbase.

Quality Content

Delivering high-quality content consistently keeps fans interested and invested in your music. Whether it's your songs, videos, or live performances, quality content is key to maintaining fan loyalty.

Community and Belonging

Creating a sense of community and belonging among your fans can foster loyalty. When fans feel like they are part of something bigger, they are more likely to stay engaged and supportive.

Wrap Up

Engaging with your audience is a vital part of building a successful music career. By leveraging modern social media platforms, maintaining authentic interactions, and offering exclusive and meaningful content, you can connect with your fans on a deeper level and build a loyal following. The techniques and ideas discussed in this chapter can help you create a strong and engaged fanbase that will support you throughout your musical journey. Remember, a loyal fan is one who feels connected, valued, and appreciated – and by focusing on these elements, you can ensure your fans keep coming back for more.

Music Videos and Visual Content

In today's fast-paced, visually-driven world, creating engaging music videos and other visual content is essential for any music artist. As consumers increasingly use their phones to access media, the demand for visually appealing content has skyrocketed. This chapter explores the importance of visual content, offers statistics on content consumption, and provides practical ideas for creating budget-friendly music videos and other visual content. We will also cover tools, current trends, and the role of artificial intelligence (AI) in producing compelling visual content that resonates with your audience.

The Need for Visual Content

The Dominance of Mobile Consumption

The way people consume media has dramatically shifted towards mobile devices. According to recent studies:

- Over 75% of global video views are on mobile devices.
- People spend an average of 2 hours and 31 minutes per day on social media, with a significant portion of that time dedicated to video content.
- Videos on social media generate 1200% more shares than text and image content combined.

These statistics highlight the importance of visual content in reaching and engaging your audience. Music videos and other visual content are powerful tools to capture attention, convey your artistic vision, and connect with fans on a deeper level.

Visual Content Ideas for Music Artists

Music Videos

Music videos are a staple in the music industry, providing a visual narrative to accompany your songs. They don't have to be expensive to be effective. With creativity and resourcefulness, you can produce captivating videos on a budget.

Lyric Videos

Lyric videos are a popular and cost-effective way to engage fans. These videos display the song's lyrics in a visually appealing manner, allowing listeners to follow along and connect with the music.

Visualisers

Visualisers are dynamic, animated graphics that react to your music. They add a visual element to your tracks without the need for extensive production. Visualisers can be used on platforms like YouTube and social media to keep your audience engaged.

Behind-the-Scenes Footage

Behind-the-scenes videos give fans a glimpse into your creative process, rehearsals, studio sessions, and everyday life as an artist. These videos build a personal connection with your audience and humanise your brand.

Live Performance Videos

Record and share your live performances. Even if it's a simple acoustic session at home or a professionally shot concert, live performance videos showcase your talent and energy. Companies like STABAL are specialists at creating cinematic and engaging live performance content. **hello@stabal.com**

Social Media Clips

Short, engaging clips for platforms like Instagram, TikTok, and Twitter can help you reach a wider audience. These can include teasers for new songs, snippets of performances, or fun, creative content related to your music.

Creating Visual Content on a Budget

Planning and Research

Before diving into production, spend time planning and researching. Define your vision, storyboard your ideas, and consider what resources you have available. Look for inspiration from other artists and identify what works well within your budget constraints.

Free and Paid Tools for Creating Visual Content

Free Tools

- **iMovie (Mac):** A user-friendly video editing tool that allows you to create and edit videos with various effects and transitions.
- **Shotcut:** A free, open-source video editor that offers a wide range of features for video editing.
- **Canva:** While primarily a graphic design tool, Canva offers video creation features that are perfect for lyric videos and social media clips.
- **DaVinci Resolve:** A professional-grade video editing software with a free version that includes powerful editing tools and effects.

Paid Tools

- **Adobe Premiere Pro:** A leading video editing software used by professionals. It offers advanced features and flexibility for creating high-quality videos.
- **Final Cut Pro (Mac):** A powerful video editing tool with a user-friendly interface, suitable for both beginners and professionals.

- **After Effects:** Ideal for creating animations, visualisers, and special effects to enhance your videos.
- **Filmora**: A budget-friendly video editing software with a range of features for creating polished videos.

DIY Music Videos

Creating a music video doesn't have to break the bank. Here are some tips to produce a professional-looking video on a budget:

- **Location:** Use visually interesting locations that are free or low-cost, such as parks, urban landscapes, or a friend's unique home.
- **Lighting:** Natural light is your best friend. Shoot during the golden hours (early morning or late afternoon) to get beautiful, soft lighting.
- **Equipment:** Use your smartphone or borrow a camera from a friend. Many modern smartphones have excellent video capabilities.
- **Editing**: Utilise free or low-cost editing software to piece together your footage. Experiment with different cuts, transitions, and effects to enhance your video.

Leveraging AI for Visual Content

AI-Driven Tools and Platforms

AI technology has revolutionised the way artists create visual content, making it easier and more affordable to produce high-quality videos and graphics. Here are some AI-driven tools and platforms that can help you create compelling visual content:

- **Lumen5:** An AI-powered video creation platform that transforms blog posts, articles, and other written content into engaging videos. It's perfect for creating social media content quickly and efficiently.

- **Animoto:** Uses AI to help you create professional videos from your photos and video clips. Its drag-and-drop interface and customisable templates make video creation simple.

- **RunwayML:** A creative suite of AI tools for generating videos, images, and other visual content. It offers features like video editing, image generation, and style transfer.

- **Magisto:** An AI-powered video editor that analyses your footage and creates polished videos with minimal effort. It's ideal for creating promotional videos and social media content.

Current Trends in AI and Visual Content

AI-Generated Music Videos

AI can assist in creating visually stunning music videos by automating parts of the production process. Tools like RunwayML can help generate unique visuals based on your music, reducing the time and cost associated with traditional video production.

Deepfake and AI Animation

Deepfake technology and AI-driven animation tools can create realistic animations and effects. These technologies are becoming more accessible, allowing artists to produce high-quality visual content without extensive resources.

Automated Editing

AI-powered editing tools like Adobe Premiere Pro's Auto Reframe and Scene Edit Detection can save time by automating repetitive tasks. These features analyse your footage and make editing suggestions based on the content, helping you create professional-looking videos faster.

Current Trends in Visual Content

Vertical Videos

With the rise of platforms like TikTok and Instagram Reels, vertical videos have become a popular format. They are optimised for mobile viewing and can increase engagement on these platforms.

Interactive Videos

Interactive videos that allow viewers to choose different paths or outcomes are becoming increasingly popular. These videos create a more engaging and immersive experience for the audience.

Behind-the-Scenes and Raw Footage

Audiences appreciate authenticity. Sharing raw, unedited footage or behind-the-scenes content can make your brand more relatable and accessible.

Animated Videos and Visualisers

Animated videos and visualisers are trendy, especially for lyric videos and social media content. They can be created with tools like After Effects or even simpler platforms like Canva and Animaker.

User-Generated Content

Encouraging fans to create and share their own content related to your music can boost engagement and reach. Repost fan-made videos, covers, and art to show appreciation and build a community.

Wrap Up

Creating engaging music videos and visual content is crucial for capturing the attention of today's mobile-focused audience. By leveraging budget-friendly tools, AI technology, and creative techniques, you can produce high-quality visual content that resonates with your fans. From music videos and lyric videos to behind-the-scenes footage and social media clips, there are numerous ways to showcase your music and build a strong visual presence. Stay current with trends, be creative, and remember that authenticity and connection are key to engaging your audience and growing your fanbase.

Email Marketing for Musicians

In this digital age, email marketing remains one of the most effective tools for musicians to communicate directly with their fans. Unlike social media platforms, which are subject to ever-changing algorithms and restrictions, email provides a direct line to your audience. This chapter explores the importance of building and using an email list, strategies for growing your list, and best practices for crafting engaging emails that keep your fans connected and engaged.

The Importance of Email Marketing

Direct Communication

Email marketing allows you to reach your fans directly in their inboxes. This direct communication channel is not influenced by social media algorithms, ensuring that your message gets seen by your subscribers.

Ownership of Your Audience

Unlike social media followers, your email list is something you own. This means you are not at the mercy of platform changes or shutdowns. Having an email list gives you control over your audience and your communication with them.

Higher Engagement Rates

Emails tend to have higher engagement rates compared to social media posts. With personalised content and targeted messaging, emails can drive more interaction, click-throughs, and conversions.

Building Your Email List

Start with Your Inner Circle

Begin by adding friends, family, and existing fans to your email list. These individuals are already invested in your music and are likely to support your efforts to grow your list.

Offer Valuable Incentives

Encourage people to join your email list by offering incentives such as exclusive content, free downloads, early access to new music, or special discounts on merchandise. Value-driven incentives can significantly boost sign-ups.

Leverage Social Media

Promote your email list on your social media channels. Share the benefits of subscribing and use call-to-action buttons and links to direct followers to your sign-up form.

Use a Sign-Up Form on Your Website

Place a prominent sign-up form on your website, ideally on the homepage or as a pop-up. Make it easy for visitors to subscribe by keeping the form simple and highlighting the benefits of joining your list.

Collect Emails at Live Events

At live performances, have a sign-up sheet or a digital device where fans can enter their email addresses. Offer incentives such as a free song download for those who sign up.

Creating Engaging Emails

Welcome Emails

Start with a warm welcome email to new subscribers. Thank them for joining your list and provide an overview of what they can expect from your emails. Include links to your social media, website, and recent music releases.

Regular Newsletters

Send regular newsletters to keep your audience updated on your latest news, upcoming releases, tour dates, and other important information. Consistency is key, so decide on a frequency that works for you (e.g., weekly, bi-weekly, monthly).

Exclusive Content

Reward your subscribers with exclusive content such as behind-the-scenes footage, early access to new songs, and special offers. This makes your email list feel valuable and encourages loyalty.

Personalised Messages

Personalise your emails by addressing subscribers by their first name and segmenting your list based on preferences and behaviour. Personalisation makes your emails feel more intimate and relevant.

Engaging Subject Lines

Craft compelling subject lines that grab attention and encourage opens. Keep them concise, intriguing, and reflective of the email's content. Avoid clickbait tactics, as they can lead to distrust.

Call-to-Actions (CTAs)

Include clear and compelling CTAs in your emails. Whether it's streaming a new song, buying concert tickets, or following you on social media, make sure your CTAs are easy to find and understand.

Best Practices for Email Marketing

Maintain a Clean List

Regularly clean your email list by removing inactive subscribers and correcting invalid email addresses. This helps maintain high deliverability rates and ensures your messages reach engaged fans. Inactive subscribers can harm your engagement metrics and increase spam complaints, so regularly review your list to keep it focused on active users. Correcting invalid email addresses helps prevent bounces and maintains your sender reputation.

Test and Optimise

Experiment with different email formats, content, subject lines, and send times. Use A/B testing to determine what resonates best with your audience and optimise your strategy accordingly. Testing allows you to understand your audience's preferences better. Try different content types, subject line styles, and send times to find the most effective combinations.

Comply with Regulations

Ensure your email marketing practices comply with regulations such as GDPR in the UK and the CAN-SPAM Act in the United States. This includes obtaining explicit consent to send emails and providing a clear unsubscribe option. Compliance is crucial for maintaining trust and avoiding legal issues. Implement a double opt-in process and regularly update your privacy policies to stay compliant.

Analyse Performance

Monitor the performance of your email campaigns by tracking open rates, click-through rates, and conversions. Use this data to refine your strategy and improve future emails. Performance analysis helps you understand what works and what doesn't. Regularly review your metrics to identify trends and adjust your strategy accordingly.

Automate Where Possible

Use email marketing software to automate repetitive tasks such as welcome emails, birthday greetings, and follow-ups. Automation saves time and ensures timely communication with your subscribers. Automated emails help maintain consistent engagement and personalisation. Set up workflows for common scenarios like new subscriber welcomes and post-purchase follow-ups to enhance your email marketing efficiency.

Recommended Email Marketing Tools

Mailchimp

Mailchimp is a popular email marketing platform that offers a range of features, including customisable templates, automation, and analytics. It has a free tier for up to 2,000 subscribers, making it an excellent choice for emerging artists.

Constant Contact

Constant Contact provides user-friendly email marketing tools with robust features such as event marketing, social media integration, and advanced reporting. It offers a 60-day free trial and various pricing plans.

Sendinblue

Sendinblue offers email marketing and SMS marketing services. It includes features like automation, segmentation, and transactional emails. Sendinblue has a free tier with limited features and competitive pricing for higher tiers.

ConvertKit

ConvertKit is designed for creators, including musicians. It offers powerful automation, tagging, and segmentation features, making it easy to deliver personalised content to your audience. ConvertKit offers a free plan for up to 1,000 subscribers.

Wrap Up

Email marketing is such an important tool for musicians to connect directly with their fans, build a loyal audience, and drive engagement. By building a robust email list, creating engaging content, and adhering to best practices, you can harness the full potential of email marketing to support your music career. Start small, experiment, and refine your strategy to see the best results. Remember, your email list is a valuable asset that, when nurtured properly, can become one of your most effective means of communication and promotion.

Networking in the Music Industry

Networking is a crucial aspect of building a successful career in the music industry. Establishing and maintaining relationships with other musicians, producers, and industry professionals can open doors to new opportunities, collaborations, and valuable insights. This chapter explores the importance of networking, provides tips for building and nurturing relationships, and offers strategies for leveraging your network to advance your music career.

The Importance of Networking in the Music Industry

Access to Opportunities

Networking connects you with individuals who can offer opportunities such as gigs, collaborations, and record deals. Building a strong network increases your visibility and enhances your chances of being considered for these opportunities.

Knowledge and Resources

Engaging with other industry professionals allows you to gain insights into the latest trends, technologies, and best practices. You can learn from their experiences and apply this knowledge to your own career.

Support System

A robust network provides emotional and professional support. Fellow musicians and industry professionals can offer advice, encouragement, and constructive feedback, helping you navigate the challenges of the music industry.

Collaboration

Networking fosters collaborations that can lead to creative growth and expanded audiences. Working with other artists and producers can result in unique projects that might not have been possible alone.

Building Relationships in the Music Industry

Attend Industry Events

Industry events such as music conferences, festivals, and workshops are excellent opportunities to meet and connect with professionals. Engage in conversations, exchange contact information, and follow up with the people you meet.

Join Professional Organisations

Becoming a member of professional organisations, such as the Recording Academy or local musicians' unions, can provide access to networking events, resources, and industry contacts.

Utilise Social Media

Social media platforms like LinkedIn, Twitter, and Instagram are powerful tools for networking. Follow industry professionals, engage with their content, and participate in relevant discussions. Platforms like LinkedIn and Twitter are particularly useful for connecting with industry professionals and staying updated on industry news.

Participate in Online Communities

Join online communities and forums dedicated to music and the music industry. Websites like Reddit, Discord, and specialised music forums can provide valuable networking opportunities and a platform to share your work and receive feedback.

Collaborate with Local Artists

Reach out to local musicians and producers for collaborations. Building relationships within your local music scene can lead to joint projects, shared gigs, and mutual support.

Volunteering and Internships

Volunteering or interning at music festivals, studios, or industry organisations can provide hands-on experience and valuable connections. These roles often lead to networking opportunities with industry professionals.

Tips for Effective Networking

Be Genuine

Authenticity is key when networking. Be yourself, show genuine interest in others, and build relationships based on mutual respect and shared interests. People are more likely to remember and appreciate you if you are sincere.

Listen and Learn

Active listening is crucial in networking. Pay attention to what others are saying, ask questions, and show interest in their experiences and perspectives. This approach helps build rapport and demonstrates your willingness to learn.

Provide Value

Offer your skills, knowledge, or resources to others in your network. Whether it's helping with a project, sharing useful information, or providing feedback, giving value can strengthen your relationships.

Follow Up

After meeting someone new, follow up with a friendly message or email. Mention something specific from your conversation to remind them of who you are. Regular follow-ups can help maintain and strengthen your connections.

Stay Consistent

Consistency is important in networking. Regularly attend events, engage on social media, and reach out to your contacts. Building a network takes time and persistence, so stay committed to the process.

Be Patient

Building a strong network doesn't happen overnight. It requires patience, effort, and time. Focus on nurturing genuine relationships rather than seeking immediate benefits.

Leveraging Your Network

Collaborative Projects

Use your network to find collaborators for projects such as songwriting, producing, or performing. Collaborative efforts can enhance your creativity, expand your reach, and lead to new opportunities.

Mentorship

Seek out mentors within your network who can provide guidance, advice, and support. Mentors can offer invaluable insights based on their experiences and help you navigate your career path.

Industry Insights

Leverage your network to stay informed about industry trends, opportunities, and challenges. Engage in conversations with industry professionals to gain a deeper understanding of the music business.

Promotional Support

Your network can help promote your music through their own channels. Ask for support in sharing your releases, gigs, and other news. Reciprocal promotion can benefit both parties and expand your audience.

Job Opportunities

Networking can lead to job opportunities in various areas of the music industry, such as session work, teaching, or working at music organisations. Stay open to diverse opportunities that can broaden your experience and skills. Volunteering or participating in an industry internship are both excellent ways to gain valuable insights and establish meaningful relationships. These experiences provide hands-on learning opportunities, allowing you to understand the intricacies of the industry while connecting with professionals who can offer guidance and support.

Tools and Platforms for Networking

LinkedIn

LinkedIn is a professional networking platform designed to help you connect with industry professionals, join relevant groups, and stay updated on the latest industry news. It offers a range of features, including professional profiles, endorsements, and recommendations, which can enhance your credibility. By actively participating in discussions, sharing industry-relevant content, and engaging with others' posts, you can build and maintain valuable professional relationships that can open doors to new opportunities and collaborations.

Instagram

Instagram is a powerful visual platform where you can showcase your work, engage with fans, and connect with industry professionals. By posting high-quality content, using relevant hashtags, and interacting through comments and direct messages, you can effectively network with other artists and professionals. Instagram Stories and Reels offer additional ways to engage your audience and provide a behind-the-scenes look at your creative process, further strengthening your online presence and connections.

X (Formerly Twitter)

X is an ideal platform for participating in industry conversations, following the latest trends, and connecting with professionals. By messaging regularly, sharing your insights, and engaging in discussions through reshares and replies, you can build a strong online presence. Following industry leaders, using relevant hashtags, and joining X chats can help you stay informed and connected with key players in your field, making X a dynamic tool for networking.

Facebook Groups

Facebook Groups dedicated to musicians and the music industry provide a valuable space for sharing information, seeking advice, and networking with peers. These groups often host discussions on industry trends, offer support and feedback, and share opportunities for collaboration.

By actively participating in group discussions, sharing your experiences, and offering help to others, you can build a supportive network of like-minded individuals and professionals.

Reddit

Reddit hosts a variety of subreddits focused on music and the music industry, such as r/music, r/musicians, and r/wearethemusicmakers. These subreddits provide a platform for participating in discussions, sharing your work, and connecting with other musicians. By contributing to conversations, asking for feedback, and sharing your knowledge, you can engage with a broad community of music enthusiasts and professionals, making Reddit a valuable tool for networking and learning.

Meetup

Meetup is a platform designed for finding and creating local events, offering a unique opportunity to connect with local musicians and industry professionals. By searching for music-related meetups in your area, you can attend events that match your interests, participate in workshops, and join jam sessions. These in-person interactions can lead to meaningful connections, collaborations, and opportunities to learn from others in your community, enhancing your professional network.

Wrap Up

Networking is an essential component of a successful music career. By building and nurturing relationships with other musicians, producers, and industry professionals, you can access new opportunities, gain valuable insights, and find support and collaboration. Approach networking with authenticity, patience, and a willingness to provide value, and you'll find that your network becomes one of your most powerful assets. Remember, the connections you make today can significantly impact your music career in the future.

Performing Live and Touring

Performing live is an amazing and essential aspect of a music career. It allows you to connect with your audience on a personal level, build a loyal fan base, and showcase your talent. Organising live shows and tours can be challenging, but whether you choose to do it yourself or work with a booking agent, understanding the process is crucial. This chapter covers everything from organising gigs, the DIY approach versus hiring a booking agent, and insider tips to make your performances as impactful as possible.

The Importance of Live Performance

Connecting with Your Audience

Live performances offer a unique opportunity to connect with your audience. The energy, emotion, and spontaneity of a live show create memorable experiences that can turn casual listeners into dedicated fans.

Building a Reputation

Consistently delivering great live shows helps build your reputation as a performer. A strong live presence can lead to more opportunities, such as opening slots for bigger acts, festival bookings, and increased media attention.

Revenue Generation

Live performances are a significant source of income. From ticket sales and merchandise to performance fees, gigs can provide essential revenue streams, especially when combined with touring.

Organising Live Shows and Tours

Doing It Yourself (DIY)

Finding Venues

Start by researching local venues that align with your music style. Reach out to venue managers with a professional email or message, including your press kit, music samples, and social media links.

Booking Shows

When booking shows, be clear about your requirements, such as sound setup, equipment, and payment terms. Be prepared to negotiate and be flexible, especially when starting out.

Promotion

Promote your gigs through social media, email newsletters, and local media. Collaborate with other artists to cross-promote each other's shows. Create eye-catching posters and flyers to distribute in local hotspots.

Planning a Tour

Planning a tour involves more logistics than individual shows. Map out potential cities and venues, considering travel distances and costs. Reach out to venues and other bands in those areas to set up a cohesive tour schedule.

Budgeting

Create a budget covering all expenses, including travel, accommodation, food, and promotional materials. Keep track of your spending to avoid going over budget.
Pros and Cons of DIY

- **Pros:** Complete control over your schedule, potential for higher profits, valuable learning experience.
- **Cons:** Time-consuming, requires significant effort and organisational skills, potential for lower initial earnings.

Finding a Booking Agent

What a Booking Agent Does
A booking agent handles the logistics of booking shows and tours, negotiating fees, and ensuring your performance needs are met. They have industry connections and experience that can open doors to better opportunities.

How to Find a Booking Agent

- **Research:** Look for agents who represent artists similar to your style and career level. Check out industry directories, attend music conferences, and network within the industry.
- **Approach:** Reach out with a professional and concise email, including your music, press kit, and a brief overview of your accomplishments and goals.
- **Referral:** Seek referrals from other musicians or industry professionals. A recommendation can go a long way in establishing credibility.

Pros and Cons of Hiring a Booking Agent

- **Pros:** Access to better opportunities, promoters/contacts, professional negotiation, saves time and effort.
- **Cons:** Agents take a commission (usually 10-20%), less control over the booking process.

Making an Impact at Gigs

Preparation and Rehearsal

Being prepared and well-rehearsed is key to a successful performance. As a booking agent for over 15 years, I've seen it all. To make an impact at a gig, you need to:

- **Rehearse Regularly:** Practice your set list thoroughly. Include transitions between songs to ensure a smooth flow.
- **Back-Up Tracks:** Have a selection of back-up tracks ready in case of technical issues or to enhance your performance.
- **Set List:** Plan your set list to build energy and keep the audience engaged. Start strong, build momentum, and finish with a memorable song.

Performance Essentials

- **Sound Check:** Arrive early for a sound check. Ensure your levels are balanced, and all equipment is functioning correctly.
- **Stage Presence:** Engage with your audience. Move around the stage, make eye contact, and interact with the crowd.
- **Merchandise:** Set up a merchandise table with your CDs, Tapes, vinyl, T-shirts, and other items. Make sure it's easily accessible and well-stocked.

Engaging with the Audience

- **Interaction:** Talk to your audience between songs. Share stories, introduce your band members, and express gratitude.

- **Audience Participation:** Encourage the audience to sing along, clap, or dance. Creating a participatory atmosphere can enhance the experience.
- **Social Media:** Encourage fans to share photos and videos of the show on social media. Use a unique hashtag to consolidate content and promote your next gigs.

Growing Your Fan Base

Performing live can come at little or no cost at the start of your journey. As you grow your fan base, release more music, and get known, your performance fee will increase. Focus on delivering quality performances consistently to build a loyal following. And make sure you always have a sign up sheet wherever you go to add new fans to your database.

Wrap Up

Performing live and touring are vital components of a successful music career. Whether you choose the DIY route or hire a booking agent, understanding the process and being well-prepared will enhance your chances of success. Remember, the key to making an impact at gigs is preparation, engagement, and consistency. As you grow your fan base and release more music, your performance opportunities and fees will naturally increase. Stay dedicated, keep refining your craft, and enjoy the experience of performing live.

Crowdfunding and Fan Support

In today's music industry, crowdfunding has emerged as a powerful tool for musicians to finance their projects, connect with fans, and create sustainable income streams. Platforms like Patreon and Kickstarter enable artists to generate funds directly from their supporters, fostering a deeper sense of community and engagement. This chapter explores the benefits of crowdfunding, provides best practices for successful campaigns, and shares personal insights on how these platforms can help music artists achieve their goals.

The Power of Crowdfunding

Direct Fan Support

Crowdfunding allows musicians to bypass traditional gatekeepers and seek support directly from their fans. This direct relationship can lead to more meaningful connections and a stronger sense of community.

Financial Independence

By leveraging the power of their fan base, musicians can fund projects without relying on record labels or loans. This financial independence enables greater creative freedom and control over their work.

Engagement and Loyalty

Crowdfunding campaigns create a unique opportunity to engage with fans on a deeper level. Supporters feel a sense of ownership and pride in contributing to your success, leading to increased loyalty and long-term support.

Sustainable Income

Platforms like Patreon allow musicians to build recurring revenue streams. By offering exclusive content and perks, artists can monetise their fan base on an ongoing basis, providing financial stability and sustainability.

Popular Crowdfunding Platforms

Patreon

Patreon is a membership platform that enables artists to receive recurring funding from their fans. Patrons subscribe to different tiers, offering monthly payments in exchange for exclusive content and rewards.

Kickstarter

Kickstarter is a project-based crowdfunding platform where artists set a funding goal and campaign duration. Backers pledge money to support the project, and funds are only collected if the campaign reaches its goal.

Indiegogo

Indiegogo is similar to Kickstarter but offers flexible funding options. This means that artists can keep the funds raised even if they don't reach their goal, providing more flexibility for smaller projects.

Best Practices for Successful Crowdfunding Campaigns

Set Clear Goals

Define specific and achievable goals for your campaign. Clearly communicate what you aim to accomplish with the funds and how supporters' contributions will be used.

Create Compelling Content

Your campaign page should include a compelling video and engaging visuals. Showcase your personality, passion, and vision. High-quality content helps build trust and excitement among potential backers.

Offer Attractive Rewards

Design reward tiers that offer real value to your supporters. Exclusive content, early access to music, personalised merchandise, and behind-the-scenes experiences are popular incentives.

Engage Your Audience

Promote your campaign through social media, email newsletters, and personal outreach. Keep your audience updated on your progress and involve them in the journey. Engagement builds momentum and encourages more contributions.

Leverage Existing Support

Mobilise your existing fan base to kickstart your campaign. Early support creates social proof and encourages others to contribute. Consider offering limited-time rewards to incentivise early backers.

Maintain Transparency

Be transparent about your progress, challenges, and successes. Regular updates and open communication build trust and keep your supporters engaged throughout the campaign.

Express Gratitude

Show appreciation for your supporters. Personalised thank-you messages, shout-outs on social media, and exclusive updates make your backers feel valued and recognised.

The Benefits of Crowdfunding for Music Artists

Creative Control

Crowdfunding empowers artists to pursue their creative vision without external interference. You retain full control over your music and projects, ensuring your work remains authentic and true to your artistic identity.

Market Validation

A successful crowdfunding campaign validates your project and demonstrates demand. This market validation can attract additional opportunities, such as media coverage, industry partnerships, and new fans.

Community Building

Crowdfunding fosters a sense of community and belonging among your supporters. By involving them in your creative process, you build a loyal and dedicated fan base that will champion your work and help spread the word.

Long-Term Support

Platforms like Patreon provide a sustainable income model, enabling you to generate ongoing support from your fans. This recurring revenue can fund future projects, cover living expenses, and provide financial stability.

Personal Connection: My Kickstarter Success Story

As a creative who has used Kickstarter, I can personally attest to the power of crowdfunding. I generated £10k for my project, which funded its creation and allowed me to monetise that asset on an ongoing basis. This support covered all of the design, development and production costs for the project. By offering exclusive content and engaging with my supporters regularly, I built a loyal community that felt invested in my success.

Steps to Launch a Successful Crowdfunding Campaign

Research and Plan

Before launching your campaign, research successful crowdfunding projects similar to yours. Learn from their strategies and plan your campaign meticulously.

Craft Your Campaign Page

Create a compelling campaign page with a clear project description, engaging visuals, and a persuasive video. Highlight the benefits of supporting your project and outline the rewards.

Set a Realistic Goal

Set a funding goal that is achievable yet ambitious enough to cover your project costs. Consider all expenses, including production, promotion, and rewards fulfilment. This may include the manufacturing of physical products or assets.

Promote Your Campaign

Leverage your existing fan base and social media channels to promote your campaign. Create a promotional plan that includes regular updates, engaging content, and calls to action.

Engage and Update

Maintain regular communication with your supporters. Provide updates on your progress, share behind-the-scenes content, and express gratitude for their contributions.

Fulfil Rewards Promptly

Deliver on your promises by fulfilling rewards promptly and accurately. High-quality rewards and timely delivery reinforce trust and satisfaction among your backers.

Wrap Up

Crowdfunding and fan support are transformative tools for musicians seeking to fund their projects, build community, and achieve financial independence. By leveraging platforms like Patreon and Kickstarter, you can engage directly with your fans, foster loyalty, and create sustainable income streams. Following best practices and maintaining a personal connection with your supporters can lead to successful campaigns and long-term success. Remember, the key to a thriving crowdfunding campaign lies in clear goals, compelling content, and genuine engagement with your audience.

Licensing and Sync Opportunities

Getting your music featured in TV shows, movies, commercials, video games, and radio shows can be a game-changer for your career. Not only does it provide significant exposure, but it can also generate substantial income. However, breaking into the world of music licensing and sync opportunities is tough and requires strategy, persistence, and understanding of the industry. In this chapter, we will explore how to navigate this complex field, share insights from my own experiences with top network TV shows, commercials, and more, and provide step-by-step guidance to help you get your music recognised.

The Benefits of Music Licensing and Sync Opportunities

Exposure

Having your music featured in popular media can significantly increase your visibility. A single placement in a hit TV show or a major commercial can introduce your music to a broad audience and attract new fans.

Revenue

Sync deals can be highly lucrative. In addition to upfront sync fees, you can earn performance royalties every time the content featuring your music is broadcasted.

Credibility

Sync placements add a level of credibility and prestige to your portfolio. Being able to showcase your work in well-known media projects can enhance your professional reputation and open more doors.

Long-Term Earnings

Music placements in TV shows, movies, and commercials often generate long-term earnings through residuals and royalties, providing a continuous revenue stream long after the initial placement.

Understanding the Industry

What is Music Licensing?

Music licensing involves granting permission to use your music in various media formats. Sync licensing, specifically, refers to synchronising music with visual media such as TV shows, films, commercials, and video games.

Types of Licenses

- **Sync License:** Allows the licensee to synchronise your music with visual content.
- **Master License:** Grants permission to use a specific recorded version of your song.
- **Mechanical License:** Required for reproducing and distributing your music in physical or digital formats.
- **Performance License:** Allows the music to be publicly performed, usually handled by performing rights organisations (PROs).

How to Get Your Music Featured

Research and Targeting

Identify the types of media where you want your music featured. Research TV shows, films, commercials, video games, and other media that align with your musical style. Pay attention to the music supervisors and production companies involved in these projects.

Do a web search on them or watch through credits to find their names.

Build a Strong Portfolio

Create a professional portfolio that includes high-quality recordings, a compelling artist bio, and a well-organised catalog of your music. Make sure your portfolio is easily accessible online.

Join a Performing Rights Organisation (PRO)

Register with a PRO like PRS for Music in the UK or if in the US then the likes of ASCAP, BMI, or SESAC. These organisations collect performance royalties on your behalf when your music is used in public performances, broadcasts, or sync placements.

Work with Music Libraries and Sync Agencies

Submit your music to reputable music libraries and sync agencies. These companies act as intermediaries between artists and media producers, helping to place your music in various media projects. Some well-known music libraries and sync agencies include:

- **Musicbed**
- **Audio Network**
- **Pond5**
- **Getty Images Music**
- **Jingle Punks**

Network with Music Supervisors

Music supervisors are responsible for selecting and licensing music for media projects. Build relationships with them by attending industry events, joining professional organisations, and reaching out via email or social media with a brief, personalised introduction and a link to your portfolio.

Leverage Online Platforms

Platforms like Songtradr, TAXI, and ReverbNation offer opportunities for artists to submit their music directly to sync opportunities. These platforms often have listings for specific projects looking for music.

Step-by-Step Guide to Getting Your Music Recognised

1. Create High-Quality Recordings
Ensure your music is professionally produced and mastered. High-quality recordings are essential for attracting the attention of music supervisors and sync agencies.

2. Organise Your Catalog
Organise your music catalog with clear metadata, including song titles, genres, moods, tempos, and keywords. This makes it easier for music supervisors to find and evaluate your tracks.

3. Register with a PRO
Sign up with a performing rights organisation to ensure you receive royalties when your music is used in media. Register each of your songs with the PRO to track their usage.

4. Research and Target Potential Opportunities
Identify media projects that align with your music style. Research the music supervisors, production companies, and music libraries involved in these projects.

5. Submit to Music Libraries and Sync Agencies
Submit your music to reputable music libraries and sync agencies. Follow their submission guidelines carefully and ensure your music is tagged with accurate metadata.

6. Build Relationships with Music Supervisors
Reach out to music supervisors with personalised emails or messages. Introduce yourself, briefly describe your music, and provide a link to your portfolio. Follow up periodically with new releases or updates.

7. Utilise Online Submission Platforms
Sign up for platforms like Songtradr, TAXI, and ReverbNation to access sync opportunities. Regularly check for new listings and submit your music to relevant projects.

8. Promote Your Successes
Share any sync placements or licensing deals on your website, social media, and press releases. Highlighting these achievements can attract more opportunities and build your credibility.

Personal Experience and Insights

As an artist who has successfully placed music with top network TV shows, commercials, video games, and radio shows, I can attest to the significant opportunities for exposure and income that sync placements provide. My experience has shown that persistence, professionalism, and networking are key to breaking into this competitive field. Keep at it and don't be too disheartened when your music isn't chosen. There is always going to be another opportunity in this thriving industry.

For instance, my track record includes placements in high-profile TV series and national advertising campaigns. These placements not only boosted my visibility but also generated substantial income through sync fees and ongoing royalties. The key to my success was a combination of building strong relationships with music supervisors, consistently submitting high-quality music, and leveraging multiple platforms to maximise my reach.

As an artist who has successfully placed music in top network TV shows, commercials, video games, and radio, I can confirm the significant opportunities for exposure and income that sync placements offer.

Persistence, professionalism, and networking are crucial to breaking into this competitive field. My placements not only boosted my visibility but also generated substantial income through sync fees and royalties. Success came from knowing my target placements, pitching to the right people, building strong relationships with music supervisors, consistently submitting high-quality music, and leveraging multiple platforms to maximise reach.

Wrap Up

Licensing and sync opportunities offer immense potential for music artists to gain exposure, generate revenue, and build a credible portfolio. This avenue allows your music to be featured in films, TV shows, commercials, video games, and other media, creating a diverse stream of income and reaching wider audiences. However, breaking into this field can be challenging.

Understanding the industry is essential. Learn the key players, such as music supervisors and sync agencies, and what they look for in tracks. Familiarise yourself with the types of licenses required and the legalities involved in music usage. Building a strong portfolio with high-quality recordings and well-organised metadata is critical. Make sure your catalog is easy to navigate and showcases your versatility.

Actively pursuing opportunities means researching potential projects and submitting your music to reputable libraries and platforms. Personalised outreach to music supervisors can also make a significant difference. Leverage your existing network and form new connections within the industry; relationships are often as important as talent in securing sync deals.

By following the steps outlined in this chapter and leveraging your network, you can position yourself for lucrative sync placements and take your music career to new heights. Remember, persistence and professionalism are your best allies in the world of music licensing and sync opportunities. Regularly update your portfolio, stay informed about industry trends, and continue refining your craft. With determination and a strategic approach, you can unlock the full potential of licensing and sync opportunities, transforming your passion into a sustainable career.

Merchandising: Beyond the Music

In the evolving landscape of the music industry, artists are increasingly diversifying their revenue streams beyond just music sales and streaming. Merchandise has become a critical component of an artist's financial portfolio. Not only does it provide an additional income source, but it also strengthens fan engagement and brand loyalty. In this chapter, we will explore the multifaceted world of merchandising, offering insights into creating, selling, and managing merchandise effectively.

The Financial Impact of Merchandise

Merchandise can significantly bolster an artist's income. For many, it constitutes a substantial portion of their earnings. Statistics show that for some artists, especially independent musicians, merchandise sales can make up 20-40% of their total income. In 2019, the global music merchandise market was valued at approximately $3.5 billion, emphasising its importance in the industry.

Types of Merchandise

When it comes to merchandise, the possibilities are vast. Here are some popular options:

- **Clothing:** T-shirts, hoodies, hats, and jackets.
- **Accessories:** Posters, stickers, patches, and pins.
- **Music:** Vinyl records, CDs, and cassette tapes.
- **Lifestyle Items:** Mugs, phone cases, tote bags, and even custom fragrances.

Designing Your Merchandise

Branding and Logo Design

Creating a cohesive and memorable brand is essential. Your merchandise should reflect your identity as an artist. Start with a distinctive logo and color scheme that aligns with your music and personal style. For example, if your music has a retro vibe, consider incorporating vintage design elements into your logo and merchandise.

Artwork for Singles or Albums

The artwork for your singles or albums can be a powerful branding tool. Use it consistently across your merchandise to create a unified aesthetic. Collaborate with graphic designers or illustrators to ensure high-quality visuals that resonate with your audience.

Finding a trusted and high-quality graphic designer to bring your ideas to life is crucial. Although it can be an expensive part of the process, the right designer can make a significant difference in whether your music gets noticed. A strong visual impact can attract new fans and help grow your audience. There are also a number of incredible online resources like www.fiverr.com to consider for all things design.

Lifestyle Brand

Consider developing a lifestyle brand that extends beyond your music. This could include apparel lines or home goods that embody your artistic persona. For instance, if you are known for eco-conscious themes, you could offer sustainable products like organic cotton T-shirts or reusable water bottles. Be creative, not everything needs to be a risk or a major cost centre as there are now so many companies that offer white labelling services or do print on demand.

Production and Fulfilment Options

Print on Demand (POD)

Print on demand services are an excellent option for minimising risk and upfront costs. Companies like Teemill, Printful, Teespring, and Redbubble allow you to create designs and only produce items when they are ordered. This means you don't need to invest in large quantities of stock and can test different designs with minimal financial risk.

Press on Demand

For music formats like vinyl or CDs, press on demand services can be very useful. Platforms like Bandcamp offer these options, allowing you to fulfill orders as they come in without holding extensive inventory. There are many options available, so it's essential to do your research. For instance, you might prefer an eco-conscious print-on-demand company. Always do your homework and don't settle for a company that doesn't feel right. Remember, you are in control.

Selling Your Merchandise

Online Stores

Setting up an online store is essential. Platforms like Shopify, Big Cartel, and WooCommerce provide user-friendly interfaces to manage your merchandise sales. Integrating your store with social media channels can also drive traffic and increase sales.

Physical Sales at Shows

Merch tables at concerts are a traditional and highly effective way to sell merchandise. Ensure your setup is visually appealing and easily accessible to attract fans. Use good lighting, clear signage, and well-organised displays to showcase your products. Consider offering exclusive items that are only available at live shows to create a sense of urgency and special value. Engage with fans personally, as a friendly interaction can significantly boost sales. Accept multiple forms of payment, including cash, cards, and mobile payments, to accommodate all customers.

Payment Options

Having a card reader is crucial for physical sales. Devices like Square, PayPal Here, and SumUp allow you to accept card payments on the go. Additionally, consider offering contactless payment options to cater to a broader audience.

Consignment

Another option is to sell your merchandise on consignment in local stores or at festivals. This approach can expand your reach and attract new fans.

Here is an example of a successful merchandising strategy

Let's look at an example of an artist who has successfully leveraged merchandise. Imagine a hypothetical indie artist, Isaac Blue, whose music blends acoustic folk with pop.

- **Brand Identity: Isaac** Blue's logo features a minimalist design with a blue gradient, reflecting the serene and modern feel of his music. This consistent and appealing branding helps Isaac stand out and makes his merchandise instantly recognisable.

- **Merchandise Line:** Isaac offers a diverse range of products, including eco-friendly T-shirts, posters featuring his album artwork, and custom guitar picks. He also includes limited-edition items like signed vinyl records and exclusive lyric booklets, which add a personal touch and create a sense of exclusivity among his fans.

- **Print on Demand:** To manage his clothing line efficiently, Isaac uses Printful, a print-on-demand service. This approach ensures that he only pays for what he sells, eliminating the risk of excess inventory and reducing upfront costs. This system allows him to experiment with new designs without significant financial risk.

- **Online Store:** Isaac's online store is powered by Shopify, which is seamlessly integrated with his Instagram and Facebook accounts. This integration makes it incredibly easy for fans to browse and purchase his merchandise directly from her social media profiles, where they already engage with his content regularly. The online store features high-quality images, detailed product descriptions, and customer reviews to enhance the shopping experience.

- **Concert Sales:** At live shows, Isaac sets up a visually appealing merch booth and uses a Square card reader to process transactions swiftly. He offers both card and contactless payment options, catering to his tech-savvy audience and ensuring a smooth purchasing experience. Additionally, He often bundles merchandise with concert tickets, offering discounts that encourage more sales.

By carefully crafting his brand and utilising efficient production and sales strategies, Isaac Blue maximises his merchandise revenue and strengthens his connection with fans. His approach not only boosts his income but also deepens fan loyalty, as his audience feels more connected to him through tangible items that represent his music and brand.

Wrap Up

Merchandise is not just an ancillary income stream; it is a vital aspect of an artist's business strategy. By understanding the various options for production, designing cohesive and appealing products, and effectively managing sales channels, artists can significantly enhance their income and deepen their relationship with their audience. As you move forward, consider how your merchandise can reflect your artistic vision and provide value to your fans, creating a lasting impact both financially and emotionally.

Well-designed merchandise serves as a tangible extension of your brand, helping to promote your music and persona even when you're not performing. It can also act as a conversation starter among fans, spreading your reach organically. Strategically timed releases, such as limited editions or tour-specific items, can create a buzz and encourage fans to act quickly, driving up sales. Furthermore, high-quality merchandise can turn casual listeners into dedicated supporters, as they feel more connected to your journey. Don't underestimate the power of well-executed merch – it's a tool for growth, loyalty, and sustainability in your career.

Mastering Music Monetisation

As the music industry continues to evolve, independent artists are presented with more opportunities than ever to generate income online. The internet has democratised access to revenue streams that were once controlled by major labels, allowing artists to reach global audiences and maximise their earnings through a strategic combination of digital distribution, royalty collection, and online marketing. This chapter will provide a guide to monetising your music, from initial distribution to unlocking revenue streams through metadata management and royalty collection.

Step 1: Distributing and Optimising Your Music

Digital Distribution Services

To make your music available on major streaming platforms and digital stores, you need a digital distribution service. Companies like DistroKid, TuneCore, and CD Baby can distribute your music to platforms like Spotify, Apple Music, Amazon Music, and more.

Steps to Get Started:

- **Choose a Distributor:** Compare services and pricing. For instance, DistroKid charges an annual fee for unlimited uploads, while TuneCore charges per release.

- **Prepare Your Music:** Ensure your tracks are mixed and mastered, and create high-quality album artwork that meets platform specifications.

- **Upload and Distribute:** Follow the distributor's instructions to upload your music, fill in metadata (e.g., song titles, artist name, genre), and select your distribution platforms.

- **Release Strategy:** Plan your release date strategically, considering pre-release promotions and setting up pre-saves on platforms like Spotify to build anticipation.

Optimising Your Streaming Profiles

Once your music is live, optimising your artist profiles on streaming platforms is crucial for maximising your reach and revenue.

Key Actions:

- **Spotify for Artists & Apple Music for Artists:** Claim your profiles, customise them with a bio, photos, and social media links, and use tools like Spotify's Artist's Pick to highlight specific tracks or playlists.

- **Playlists:** Submit your music to official playlists, reach out to independent playlist curators, or create your own playlists to include your music alongside similar artists.

Step 2: Selling Downloads, Physical Copies, and Leveraging Online Sales Platforms

Digital Downloads and Physical Copies

While streaming is dominant, selling digital downloads and physical copies can still be lucrative.

Platforms to Consider:

- **Bandcamp:** Ideal for selling digital downloads and physical copies, allowing you to set your own prices and offer fans the option to pay more.

- **iTunes/Amazon:** Ensure your music is available on major digital stores through your distributor.

- **Physical Copies:** Use services like Cram Duplication or Kunaki for CDs and Disc Makers for vinyl production. Offer merch bundles to increase sales.

Direct-to-Fan Sales and Crowdfunding

Selling directly to your fans and crowdfunding can be more profitable by eliminating middlemen.

Key Platforms:

- **Shopify & Bandcamp:** Create an online store for selling downloads, physical copies, and merchandise.

- **Crowdfunding:** Use Kickstarter or Patreon to fund your next project, offering exclusive rewards to backers and building a community of supporters.

Step 3: Maximising Royalties with Metadata and ISRC Codes

The Importance of Metadata

Metadata is the hidden information within your music files that ensures your music is properly identified and tracked across platforms, making it possible for you to earn royalties.

Best Practices:

- **Accurate Metadata:** Enter all required metadata meticulously when uploading your music, and use consistent naming conventions to avoid confusion.

- **Regular Updates:** Regularly check and update your metadata, especially if you re-release music or make changes to your brand.

Understanding ISRC Codes

The International Standard Recording Code (ISRC) is a unique identifier assigned to each of your recordings, essential for tracking your music and ensuring you receive royalties.

How to Obtain and Use ISRC Codes:

- **Obtaining Codes:** ISRC codes can be obtained through your digital distributor or a national ISRC agency. Ensure your tracks are correctly coded.

- **Usage:** ISRC codes are embedded in your music's metadata and are used across streaming platforms, digital stores, radio stations, and physical copies to track and credit your music accurately.

Step 4: Earning and Collecting Royalties

Types of Royalties

Comprehending the various categories of royalties that you have the potential to earn is crucial for effectively maximizing your overall income and ensuring that you capture every possible revenue stream.

Main Types:

- **Mechanical Royalties:** Earned from the reproduction of your music, such as sales, downloads, and streaming.

- **Performance Royalties:** Generated when your music is performed publicly, whether on radio, TV, or live venues.

- **Sync Licensing Royalties:** Paid when your music is used in visual media like films, TV shows, or advertisements.

How to Collect Royalties

To collect your royalties, you need to be registered with the appropriate collection agencies.

Steps to Follow:

- **Join a Performance Rights Organisation (PRO):** Sign up with a PRO like PRS for Music (UK), ASCAP, SESAC or BMI (US) to track public performances and collect royalties.

- **Register with a Mechanical Rights Agency:** In the UK, the MCPS handles mechanical royalties, while in the US, services like Harry Fox Agency or Music Reports are key players.

- **Digital Distributors:** Platforms like TuneCore, DistroKid, or CD Baby can handle the complex process of royalty collection for streaming services and digital stores.

Step 5: Marketing, Promotion, and Licensing Opportunities

Marketing and Promotion

A strong online presence drives traffic to your music, enhancing your earning potential.

Strategies:

- **Website & Email Marketing:** Create a professional website and build an email list to keep fans informed about new releases, tours, and exclusive offers.

- **Targeted Advertising:** Use social media and Google Ads to reach specific audiences, and consider streaming platform ads to directly reach potential listeners.

Licensing and Sync Opportunities

Licensing your music for use in TV, films, commercials, and video games can be highly lucrative.

Key Approaches:

- **Sync Agencies & Direct Submissions:** Work with agencies like Musicbed (US) or Pitch & Sync (UK) and use platforms like Songtradr for direct submissions to media producers.

Wrap Up

Monetising your music online requires a strategic approach, attention to detail, and consistent effort. By effectively distributing your music, optimising your streaming presence, managing your metadata and ISRC codes, and strategically promoting your work, you can create multiple revenue streams that sustain your career. Moreover, understanding and collecting royalties through the correct channels ensures that your hard work is compensated. Stay adaptable, continuously refine your strategies, and be responsive to your audience's preferences to build a thriving music career in the digital age.

Financial Management for Independent Artists

Managing finances effectively is so important for independent artists who often have to juggle multiple income streams and expenses. Good financial management can provide stability and allow for strategic growth in your career. This chapter will cover budgeting, managing income, and recommend tools to help streamline these processes.

Budgeting

Creating a Budget

A budget is a financial plan that helps you allocate your income towards various expenses, savings, and investments. Here's how to create a budget:

Track Your Income: Identify all your income sources, including music sales, streaming revenue, merchandise, live performances, and any other side gigs.

List Your Expenses: Categorise your expenses into fixed (rent, utilities, insurance) and variable (travel, marketing, equipment). Don't forget to include savings and emergency funds.

Set Financial Goals: Define short-term and long-term financial goals, such as saving for an album release or funding a tour.

Allocate Funds: Assign portions of your income to each expense category. Ensure your spending aligns with your financial goals.

Free Budgeting Tools

Google Sheets: Create customised budgeting templates to track your income and expenses.
Mint: An intuitive app that links to your bank accounts, categorises transactions, and provides budget insights.

Paid Budgeting Tools

YNAB (You Need A Budget): A comprehensive budgeting tool that encourages proactive financial planning. Costs about £75 per year.
QuickBooks Self-Employed: Excellent for managing business expenses and income, costing around £15 per month.

Managing Income

Diversifying Income Streams

Relying solely on one income source can be risky. Diversifying your income streams not only spreads risk but also enhances stability and financial security. Here are key strategies to consider:

Music Sales and Streaming: Continuously release new music across various platforms and actively promote your releases to expand your audience and increase revenue.

Merchandise: Create and sell branded merchandise both online and at live events. Engage with your fan base through exclusive items that resonate with your brand.

Live Performances: Secure gigs, tours, and explore opportunities for live-streaming performances to supplement your income. Utilise platforms that connect artists with virtual audiences globally.

Licensing and Royalties: License your music for use in TV shows, films, commercials, and video games. Explore partnerships with sync agencies and platforms that facilitate music placements.

Teaching and Workshops: Offer music lessons, workshops, or masterclasses to share your skills and knowledge. This can be a rewarding income stream while fostering community engagement and building your reputation as an artist.

By diversifying your income through these channels, you can create a more sustainable financial foundation and broaden your opportunities within the music industry, whether you're based in the UK, USA, or elsewhere.

Tracking Income

Effectively tracking your income is essential for financial stability and accurate accounting. Key strategies include:

Separate Accounts:

Personal vs. Business Accounts: Maintain separate bank accounts for personal and business finances to simplify tracking, ensure clarity, and manage expenses and income efficiently.
Benefits: Clearer financial records and simplified accounting.

Invoicing:

Creating and Managing Invoices: Use invoicing tools for performances, teaching sessions, merchandise sales, and other services to ensure timely payments and professional client relationships.

Recommended Tools:

Wave: A free tool offering invoicing, expense tracking, and basic accounting, ideal for beginners.

FreshBooks: Starting at $15 per month, FreshBooks provides robust invoicing and accounting services for more established artists.

Free Income Management Tools

Wave:

Features: Free invoicing, expense tracking, and basic accounting. Links to bank accounts, categorises transactions, and provides financial overviews.

Benefits: Comprehensive and cost-effective.

HoneyBook:

Features: Free trial with client bookings, contracts, and payments. Integrates project management with financial tracking.

Benefits: Simplifies client interactions and financial management.

Paid Income Management Tools

FreshBooks:

Features: Starting at $15 per month, it offers invoicing, expense tracking, time tracking, and financial reporting. Supports client management and integrates with payment gateways.

Benefits: Comprehensive and scalable.

Xero:

Features: Starting at $11 per month, it includes invoicing, expense tracking, payroll management, and financial reporting. Integrates with numerous third-party apps.

Benefits: Versatile and suitable for detailed financial management.

Leveraging these tools and strategies ensures accurate financial records, streamlined accounting processes, and timely payments, whether in the UK, USA, or elsewhere.

When Do I Give Up My Day Job to Become a Full Time Artist?

Pursuing a career in music is a dream for many, but knowing when to leave the security of a day job can be daunting. The journey to becoming a full-time musician requires careful planning, financial stability, and sometimes, a leap of faith. This chapter explores a dual approach: working within the music industry while balancing a day job, and recognising when it's the right time to fully commit to your music career.

Balancing a Day Job with Music

Working Within the Music Industry

Maintaining financial stability while pursuing your passion for music is achievable by finding employment within the music industry. This approach allows you to stay connected to your artistic aspirations while earning a steady income. Here are some roles that can complement your journey as a music artist:

Music Teacher or Vocal Coach: Sharing your knowledge and skills with students not only provides a steady income but also enhances your understanding and mastery of music. Teaching can be fulfilling and helps you stay immersed in the music world.

Session Musician: Working as a session musician allows you to play with various artists and bands. This role provides valuable experience, expands your repertoire, and offers networking opportunities that can lead to further gigs and collaborations.

Sound Engineer or Producer: Developing technical skills in sound engineering or music production can open doors to studio work and collaborations. These roles are crucial in the music creation process and offer diverse career paths within the industry.

Music Journalist or Blogger: Writing about music keeps you engaged with the industry and helps you build connections with other professionals. It also sharpens your analytical skills and deepens your appreciation of different music styles and trends.

Music Retail or Instrument Repair: Jobs in music stores or instrument repair shops keep you close to the latest gear and trends in the industry. This work can provide insights into the practical aspects of musicianship and gear maintenance.

By working within the music industry, you can financially support your artistic endeavors while continuing to grow and network in your field. This dual approach ensures you remain connected to your passion and stay informed about industry developments.

Knowing When to Go Full-Time

Transitioning to a full-time music career requires careful planning and a solid financial foundation. Here are some indicators that you might be ready to make the leap:

Financial Stability and Income Streams

Regular Income from Music: If you're consistently earning from music releases, live performances, and merchandise sales, it indicates a stable revenue stream. This consistent income can provide the financial security needed to transition to full-time.

Paid Gigs: A steady schedule of paid gigs provides reliable income and suggests that your music is in demand. Regular performances also help build your reputation and fan base.

Merchandise Sales: Strong merchandise sales can significantly boost your income. If your fans are regularly buying your merch, it's a good sign of a dedicated fan base willing to support you financially.

Crowdfunding Support: Platforms like Patreon can provide a steady income through fan support. If your Patreon earnings cover your living expenses, it may be time to consider going full-time. This model allows fans to directly contribute to your career.

Risk and Motivation

It's important to recognise that going full-time in music is a risk. The biggest risk-takers are often the most motivated and driven, but it's crucial not to jump in too soon. Here are some factors to consider:

Savings and Financial Cushion: Ensure you have savings to fall back on during lean times. A financial cushion can help you navigate the ups and downs of a music career, providing peace of mind and stability.

Support System: Having a supportive network of family, friends, or a partner can make the transition smoother. Their encouragement and understanding can be invaluable during challenging times.

Business Plan: Treat your music career like a business. Have a clear plan for how you will generate income and sustain your career in the long run. This plan should include marketing strategies, financial goals, and a timeline for achieving milestones.

By assessing these factors and preparing thoroughly, you can make a more informed decision about transitioning to a full-time music career. This approach increases your chances of long-term success and fulfillment in the music industry.

Wrap Up

Deciding when to give up your day job and focus solely on music is a deeply personal decision. It requires a careful balance of passion, financial stability, and readiness to take risks. By working within the music industry, you can stay connected to your passion while building a stable foundation. When your music career generates enough income to support you, and you have the motivation and resources to take the leap, you'll know it's the right time to commit fully to your dream.

Remember, every artist's journey is unique. Some find success quickly, while others take a longer path. Trust in your process, stay dedicated, and keep pushing forward. Your time will come.

Sustaining Long-Term Success

Achieving success in the music industry is a significant milestone, but maintaining that success over the long term requires a different set of skills and strategies. This chapter will provide tips for maintaining momentum, evolving as an artist, and avoiding burnout.

Maintaining Momentum

Consistent Content Creation

Regular Releases: Keep your audience engaged by regularly releasing new music. Whether it's singles, EPs, or full albums, maintaining a consistent release schedule helps keep you in the public eye.

Engage with Fans: Use social media, newsletters, and live interactions to stay connected with your fan base. Regular updates and behind-the-scenes content can keep your audience invested in your journey.

Collaborations: Working with other artists can introduce you to new audiences and provide fresh creative inspiration. Seek out collaborations that align with your artistic vision and expand your reach.

Strategic Planning

Set Goals: Establish short-term and long-term goals for your music career. Having clear objectives helps you stay focused and motivated.

Plan Tours and Events: Live performances are crucial for building a loyal fan base. Plan your tours and events strategically to maximise exposure and revenue.

Monitor Industry Trends: Stay informed about changes in the music industry. Understanding market trends can help you adapt and seize new opportunities.

Evolving as an Artist

Continuous Learning

Expand Your Skills: Continuously improve your musical skills by learning new instruments, experimenting with different genres, or honing your production abilities.

Stay Curious: Explore new sounds, technologies, and artistic influences. Staying curious and open to experimentation can lead to innovative and exciting music.

Seek Feedback: Constructive feedback from trusted peers and mentors can provide valuable insights and help you grow as an artist.

Rebranding and Reinvention

Fresh Visuals: Update your visual branding periodically. New album art, logos, and merchandise designs can reinvigorate your image and attract attention.

Explore New Themes: Evolve your lyrical content and themes to reflect your personal growth and changing perspectives. This keeps your music relevant and relatable.

Adapt to Change: Be willing to adapt your style and approach as the music landscape changes. Artists who evolve with the times remain relevant and successful.

Avoiding Burnout

Balance and Self-Care

Set Boundaries: Establish boundaries between your work and personal life. Taking regular breaks and setting aside time for non-musical activities can prevent burnout.

Practice Self-Care: Prioritise your mental and physical health. Exercise, meditation, and spending time with loved ones are essential for maintaining well-being.

Delegate Tasks: Don't try to do everything yourself. Delegate tasks such as marketing, management, and production to trusted team members or professionals.

Sustainable Work Habits

Manage Your Time: Develop effective time management skills. Create a balanced schedule that allows for creativity, business tasks, and rest.

Set Realistic Goals: Avoid overcommitting yourself. Set achievable goals and recognise that it's okay to take things one step at a time.

Celebrate Milestones: Acknowledge and celebrate your achievements, no matter how small. Recognising your progress can boost morale and keep you motivated.

Wrap Up

Sustaining long-term success in the music industry requires dedication, adaptability, and a focus on well-being. By maintaining momentum through consistent content creation and strategic planning, evolving as an artist, and prioritising self-care to avoid burnout, you can build a lasting and fulfilling career.

Remember, the journey is just as important as the destination. Stay true to your passion, remain open to growth, and continue to find joy in your music. With the right mindset and strategies, you can sustain your success and enjoy a long and vibrant career in the music industry.

Navigating the Noise: How to Make Smart Choices in a Tough Industry

Introduction

The music industry is filled with dreams, opportunities, and promises. It's a place where success stories seem to happen overnight, and where the next "big thing" is just a click away. As an independent artist, you're entering an exciting and vibrant world, but also one that can be filled with traps and challenges that can cost you—both financially and emotionally.

From overpriced marketing schemes to empty promises of quick fame, it's easy to be persuaded to spend your hard-earned money where it won't give you the return you're hoping for. Over my 20+ years in this industry, I've seen artists thrive, but I've also seen far too many fall victim to the pitfalls that lie in wait for the unwary. In this chapter, I want to arm you with the wisdom to make good decisions, the kind that will protect your career and keep your finances in check.

Beware of the "Get-Famous-Quick" Scams

One of the biggest traps in the industry is the idea that success can happen overnight if you just spend enough money. Social media is filled with ads promising thousands of streams, instant followers, and label attention. These can be tempting when you're just starting out, but trust me when I say that the vast majority of these services are scams. Most of them offer nothing but inflated numbers that don't translate into real fans, engagement, or money. Buying followers or streams won't make you successful; building an authentic connection with your audience will.

I've worked with artists who were seduced by these promises. After spending thousands on fake streams and bot followers, they were left with empty accounts and no real progress in their careers. Don't be one of them.

Spend Your Money Where It Counts

One of the biggest challenges for independent artists is knowing where to invest their money. It's easy to throw cash at a flashy PR company or expensive gear, but not all of these investments will move the needle. Instead, spend money on things that will truly benefit your growth—like high-quality recordings, engaging visuals, and most importantly, your own education. Learning how to market yourself effectively can often be more valuable than paying someone else to do it for you.

I've seen artists invest in pricey PR campaigns before they had a solid brand or following. The result? They didn't get the attention they hoped for, and the money was wasted. Build the foundation first, and then invest wisely in promotion once you're ready.

Don't Believe the Social Media Hype

Social media has become a double-edged sword for musicians. On one hand, it's a powerful tool to connect with fans, promote your music, and grow your audience. On the other hand, it can also be a breeding ground for unrealistic expectations and misinformation. The polished images and viral success stories you see online are rarely the full picture. Don't compare your journey to someone else's highlight reel, and don't let the pressure of keeping up push you into making rash decisions.

I've seen artists get discouraged because they didn't reach 10,000 followers in a month, or because their song didn't go viral. The truth is, these things take time, effort, and consistency. Social media success should be seen as a byproduct of good work, not the goal itself.

Work with People You Trust

The music industry is built on relationships, and who you work with matters. There are countless "professionals" out there who will promise to help you break through, but not all of them have your best interests at heart. Before signing contracts, hiring a manager, or even paying for services, do your research. Look for people with a proven track record, and more importantly, trust your gut. If something feels off, it probably is.

I've worked with artists who rushed into management deals, only to find themselves locked into contracts that didn't serve them. It's always better to take your time finding the right people than to end up tied to someone who isn't helping you grow.

Education is Key

One of the best investments you can make as an independent artist is in your own education. The more you know about the industry—whether it's about royalties, licensing, or marketing—the better equipped you'll be to make informed decisions. Don't be afraid to take courses, read books, and ask questions. The more knowledge you have, the harder it will be for anyone to take advantage of you.

Over the years, I've seen the most successful independent artists be the ones who are constantly learning. They're the ones who take the time to understand how the business side works, and as a result, they're able to make smarter choices and protect their careers.

Wrap Up

The music industry can be a tough place to navigate, especially as an independent artist. There are plenty of people out there who will try to sell you the dream, but not all of them will help you get there. By staying grounded, making informed decisions, and investing in yourself, you can avoid many of the pitfalls that have tripped up so many others.

Remember, success in this industry is a marathon, not a sprint. It takes time, dedication, and patience to build a sustainable career. There will be moments of frustration, and times when you feel like you're being pulled in multiple directions. But by arming yourself with the right knowledge, surrounding yourself with trustworthy people, and always keeping your long-term vision in focus, you can protect both your career and your wallet.

In the end, it's not just about how much money you invest or who you know—it's about staying true to your artistry while making smart, strategic moves. Don't be afraid to ask questions, seek out mentors, and continuously educate yourself about the business. The more you know, the more empowered you'll be to steer your own path in an industry that can often feel overwhelming.

Most importantly, trust the process. Growth takes time, and every lesson you learn along the way—whether it comes from success or failure—will shape you into a stronger, wiser artist. Protect your career by being cautious but also confident in your ability to carve out your place in this industry. Keep creating, keep learning, and remember that each step forward is progress, no matter how small.

Ultimately, the music industry is about longevity. You don't want to burn out chasing quick wins or empty promises. By making thoughtful, calculated decisions and being mindful of where and how you invest your time, money, and energy, you'll be able to build a career that isn't just profitable but also fulfilling. Stay patient, trust your journey, and let your passion guide you, but always with your eyes wide open.

Building Your Dream Team

Introduction

As an independent artist, you've likely spent a lot of time wearing many hats: songwriter, producer, promoter, accountant, and more. While this level of involvement can give you a well-rounded understanding of the music industry, there will come a point in your career when the demand for your time, energy, and creativity becomes too great to manage alone. This is when you should begin to consider building a team around you—a group of professionals who can help you elevate your career to the next level and allow you to focus on what truly matters: your music. Building a team isn't about losing control; it's about strategically delegating responsibilities to experts who can help you grow in ways you can't do on your own. The right team will provide you with the freedom to create while ensuring that all the logistical, financial, and legal aspects of your career are handled by people who know their stuff. You'll know when the time is right because you'll find yourself spending more time on admin and logistical tasks than on the creative work that got you here in the first place.

So, who should be part of your dream team?

The Mentor: Your Compass and Sounding Board

As your career gains traction, having a mentor can be invaluable. A mentor is someone who has walked a similar path and can offer guidance, advice, and perspective. This person isn't necessarily part of your day-to-day operations, but they provide an outside perspective that can help you navigate tricky situations, set goals, and avoid potential pitfalls. A mentor will also help keep you grounded when things get overwhelming, reminding you why you started in the first place.

When looking for a mentor, seek someone who genuinely understands your vision and values. They should be someone you respect, who has a track record of success, and who is willing to invest time in helping you grow.

The Accountant: Keeping Your Finances in Check

The music industry is full of stories about artists who made it big but ended up with nothing because they didn't manage their finances properly. As your career grows, so will your income streams—from royalties and merch sales to performance fees and streaming revenue. Managing this income and ensuring that you're setting aside enough for taxes, reinvesting in your career, and securing your future is critical.

An accountant who specialises in working with artists or freelancers can be a game-changer. They'll help you keep track Building of your income and expenses, create a financial plan, and make sure you're compliant with tax laws. Most importantly, they'll free up your time to focus on your music, without worrying about whether you're handling your finances correctly.

The Lawyer: Protecting Your Interests

As your career grows, you'll be faced with contracts, licensing agreements, and other legal documents that require careful consideration. Having a lawyer who specialises in entertainment law is essential to ensure that you're protected in every deal you make. Whether you're signing with a label, licensing your music for film or TV, or negotiating a sponsorship deal, a lawyer will help you navigate the legal language, protect your rights, and secure the best possible terms.

Don't underestimate the importance of having a good lawyer in your corner. They'll help you avoid costly mistakes and ensure that you retain control of your work.

The Manager: Your Career Architect

Once you reach a certain level of success, managing your day-to-day career becomes increasingly complex. Booking shows, negotiating deals, marketing your brand, and maintaining relationships all require constant attention. This is where a manager comes in. A good manager will help you develop a long-term strategy for your career, handle negotiations, and coordinate the many moving parts of your professional life. However, choosing a manager is one of the most important decisions you'll make. They need to be someone you trust implicitly and who genuinely believes in your vision. The right manager will act as your biggest advocate, helping you make the best decisions for your career while keeping you focused on your goals.

The Live Agent: Securing Opportunities to Perform

A live agent is responsible for booking your shows and negotiating performance fees. As live performance continues to be one of the most significant revenue streams for independent artists, having someone dedicated to securing opportunities for you to perform is critical.
A live agent will know the market, have the right contacts, and be able to secure the best opportunities for your career. Whether it's small club gigs, festival spots, or opening for a major act, your live agent will ensure that your live presence continues to grow.

Other Key Roles: Publicist, Distributor, and More
Depending on the growth of your career, you may eventually want to expand your team further. A publicist can help you manage your media presence and build your brand. A distributor can ensure your music reaches the right platforms in the best possible way. You might also want to bring on a tour manager, merchandiser, or social media strategist.

The key is to build your team at a pace that feels right for you. Start with the roles that are most essential to your growth and add others as needed.

Wrap Up

Building a team isn't something you need to rush into, but it is a critical step in the evolution of your career. The right team will help you maximize your potential, handle the responsibilities that are outside of your expertise, and ensure that you can stay focused on creating great music. You'll know it's time to expand when the admin, legal, and financial aspects of your career start taking up more of your time than your creative work.

At the end of the day, your team should support your vision and values, working together to help you achieve your long-term goals. It's a reflection of your growth as an artist and a necessary part of building a sustainable, profitable career. So when the time is right, embrace the idea of sharing the load and letting your team help you take your career to the next level.

Embracing the Journey of an Independent Artist

As we reach the end of this book, I want to take a moment to reflect on the incredible journey you're about to embark on—or perhaps are already navigating. Being an independent artist is both a challenging and rewarding path, full of unique experiences, opportunities for growth, and countless moments of personal and professional development.

When I began my journey, I envisioned a future solely as an artist, pouring my heart and soul into creating and performing music. But as time went on, I discovered a deep passion for helping others achieve their dreams. This led me down a different path, one that involved management and becoming a booking agent. This unexpected turn showed me that the music industry is vast and full of opportunities, many of which I had never considered when I first started.

Your path as an independent artist will be uniquely your own. Whether you're just starting out or have been on this journey for a while, each chapter of this book is designed to provide guidance and encouragement to help you make positive strides forward. From learning how to effectively promote your music and engage with fans, to understanding the intricacies of music production and distribution, every step you take is a step towards realising your full potential.

It's important to remember that success in the music industry doesn't always follow a linear path. You might find yourself exploring different roles and discovering new passions along the way. Perhaps you'll delve into songwriting for other artists, producing, or even teaching and mentoring the next generation of musicians. Each experience will enrich your journey and contribute to your growth.

This book aims to be a resource and a companion for you, offering insights and strategies to navigate the challenges and seize the opportunities that come your way. I hope the chapters on recording cover songs, balancing a day job with your music career, and sustaining long-term success have provided you with practical advice and inspiration. Remember, it's about finding what works for you and embracing the process, no matter how unconventional it may seem.

Your journey as an independent artist is a testament to your passion, resilience, and dedication. It's a journey that requires courage to take risks, the willingness to learn and adapt, and the perseverance to keep moving forward even when the road gets tough. But it's also a journey filled with creativity, joy, and the fulfillment of turning your dreams into reality.

As you continue on this path, stay true to your artistic vision and keep pushing your boundaries. Celebrate your successes, learn from your setbacks, and always remain open to new opportunities and experiences. Your unique voice and perspective are what make your music special, and the world is waiting to hear it.

Thank you for allowing me to be a part of your journey through this book. I hope it has helped you discover new areas to develop, given you the tools to navigate the industry, and, most importantly, encouraged you to believe in yourself and your potential. Your journey is yours to shape, and I'm excited for all the incredible things you will achieve.

Start today, keep going, and never stop chasing your dreams. The music industry is ready for you, and there's no limit to what you can accomplish as an independent artist.

Beyond The Book

Continue Your Journey

Thank you for taking the time to read "The Indie Artist Playbook." I hope it has provided you with valuable insights and practical advice to help you on your journey as an independent artist. However, the journey doesn't have to end here. If you'd like to connect with me for more personalised input and guidance, I offer consultation services to help you take your music career to the next level.

For information on consultations, you can contact me through: **www.dougross.co.uk**

A Bit More About Me

I'm Doug Ross, a husband and father of four, based on the south coast of England. Currently, I serve as the CEO of STABAL, a film and production company that has filmed hundreds of music artists, including Craig David, Kid Rock and Gary Numan, to name a few. You can check out some of the incredible videos we've created for independent artists on our YouTube channel. **www.youtube.com/@stabal**

Despite my busy schedule, I still manage to DJ around the world under the name **Kubiks**, performing about 50 shows a year, and continue to produce and release drum and bass music. Life is certainly a juggle, but I believe in seizing every moment, grabbing every opportunity, and enjoying every minute.

You can listen to my latest tracks and connect with me on social media through the following link: **www.linktr.ee/kubiks**

Thank you again for your support. Let's continue to make amazing music and turn our artistic dreams into reality.

Printed in Great Britain
by Amazon